Some Comments on CUBA TODAY

"A three-month visit in the autumn of 1971 and a return trip in March and April of 1975 provided Englishwoman Chadwick with opportunities to observe what very few Americans have seen in recent years: Cuba. Quite open-mindedly, she examines the effects of Castro's regime on the fabric of socioeconomic life, particularly as it concerns young people." — ALA BOOKLIST

"an accessible and informative book" — THE KIRKUS SERVICE

"Having just returned from a week's visit in Cuba... I found Lee Chadwick's CUBA TODAY an exciting, accurate and hopeful interpretation of a people who have been so long insulated and isolated from many of us in the United States...This book serves as a bridge between two peoples who need one another very much." — BRUCE L. JONES, *Department of Christian Education, Christian Church Division of Homeland Ministries (Director of Education)*

"Aspects of Cuban life are approached with a thoroughness that is appealing as well as informative. The most unique areas deal with Chadwick's incorporation into Cuban life. She visits homes and describes them; travels throughout the country-side visiting historical places including Oriente, the birthplace of the revolution, and describes various neighborhoods, as well as landscapes and architecture. The reader is able to escort her as she rides a crowded bus, visits museums and monuments and joins other Sunday picknickers at a local park. This is what makes the book valuable — it answers questions that many experts tend to overlook. Chadwick does not seek to analyze life in Cuba but chooses instead to live. A feeling of Cuban life is acquired that could only be matched by a visit to the island." — THE GUARDIAN

'Work.' Cartoon drawn by pupils of Vento Secondaria, Cuba's first vocational school (page 101).

CUBA TODAY

by

Lee Chadwick

LAWRENCE HILL & COMPANY

Westport, Connecticut

Library of Congress Catalog Card Number: 75–43185
ISBN: 0–88208–065–2

Published in the United States
by permission of Dobson Books Ltd

September, 1977, first paperback edition

Lawrence Hill & Co., Publishers, Inc.

Manufactured in the United States of America
by Ray Freiman & Company

'That is how we want the children of our America to be: men who say what they think and say it well: sincere and eloquent men.'—José Martí, *The Golden Age*.

FOREWORD

THIS IS a traveller's view of Cuba with all the limitations that implies. It is also a partisan view because consciously or unconsciously every traveller looks most closely at what interests them most. In my case it was children, and Cuba's young people are good ambassadors for their country.

Cuba has suffered from a few visitors from developed countries who managed to leave the impression that they thought they could have run Cuba's revolution much better themselves. This maybe is why some have received a dusty answer.

As to my own experience, I should like to express sincere thanks for invaluable aid and much kindness received in a three months' personal quest to learn more about Cuba and its children.

While conversations are from detailed notes taken at the time, any errors or misconceptions that may have crept in from language difficulties or other causes are entirely my responsibility.

Many thanks to the Foreign Press department of the Cuban Ministry of Foreign Relations and to the Cuban Embassy in London for photographs. Parts of the chapter "Schooling the Whole Man" first appeared in the *Times Educational Supplement*. The quotations from *The Autobiography of a Runaway Slave* by Esteban Montejo, edited by Miguel Barnet (copyright © 1968 by the Bodley Head, Ltd) are reprinted by permission of Pantheon Books, a division of Random House, Inc.

FLORIDA

GULF OF
MEXICO

Havana   Matanzas

PINAR DEL RIO   HABANA

Pinar del Rio   MATANZAS   SantaC

LAS VILL

ISLE
OF
PINES   Bay of Pigs   Cienfuegos

Trinidad

Escambray

Sancti Sp

CARIBBEAN

CUBA

0   100   200

CONTENTS

Foreword   *page* 7
Map of Cuba by Peter Martin   *page 8–9*

Part I

BACKGROUND TO THE NEW CUBA

Four hundred years of Spanish colonial rule   13
   Farming traditions in Cuba – Effects of the French and American Revolutions – The 1868 rising and the Ten Years' War – José Martí 1853-1895 – The War of Independence 1895-1898

The rise and fall of a republic   33
   The generation of the 'thirties – The rise of Batista – Fidel Castro and a new Cuban generation – The Moncada attack – 'History will absolve me'

Guerrilla war   48
   The Granma expedition – The revolutionary organisations – The city resistance – Total war

From national liberation to socialism   59
   Invasion as Cuba goes socialist

Part II

HAVANA DIARY

First impressions   69
   A school for peasant girls – An evening visit

Table talk 78

Fair shares – 'There are no little blacks, nor little whites – only Cubans.' Antonio Maceo – *One man's testimony – Brief encounter*

Recollections of the literacy campaign 91

Schooling the whole man–cuba's educational revolution 96

School in the countryside – Vocational schools – An assessment – Two primary schools – Recent developments in Cuba's educational revolution

A grass roots organisation 114

Neighbourhood committees – A People's Court

Rebel youth 121

Sundays in Havana 125

Cathedral Square – Havana's museums – The harbour side

Children's literature in Cuba 135

A conversation resumed

The arts in a changing Society 144

A Cuban language in cinema – Ballet for everybody – 'You may graft the world cultural heritage to the tree of our republics, but let the trunk continue to be that of our republics.'—José Martí

Part III

THE DEVELOPING COUNTRYSIDE

Farewell Havana 153

In Matanzas Province – A citrus fruit plan – A fishing school – History of a marsh

In Las Villas. ancient and modern   162
Where time has stood still – Teacher training on a mountain top

Farming in Camagüey   170
A sugar town – Lessons learnt – Making the sugar – A celebration – Mechanising the sugar harvest – The Youth Columns of Camagüey – The Dairy Triangle of Camagüey – Life on a pineapple farm

In Oriente, cradle of the revolution   183
Conversation in Holguin – Care of the pre-school child – From Bayamo to Santiago – Heroic city – The University of Oriente – A family code – Retracing history: from Moncada to Sierra

Postscript   202
Cuba revisited – A last look at Santiago

PART I
Background To The New Cuba

FOUR HUNDRED YEARS OF SPANISH COLONIAL RULE

MOST ACCOUNTS of Cuba's past tend to begin with her 'discovery' but, like Prospero's isle, Cuba had her own life style long before the stranger came and claimed her 'in the name of Christ, Our Lady and the reigning monarchs of Spain'.

On the Sunday in October nearly five hundred years ago (1492) when the explorer Christopher Columbus found Cuba and, just beyond, a new continent, the island must have been looking its green and smiling best for he considered it the most beautiful place human eyes had ever seen. It was blessed with a fertile soil but gold it contained only in small traces though later prospectors found other metals: nickel and copper, iron and manganese.

Much of Cuba consists of plains and gentle slopes, so that with the abundance of good soil, more than half of the island is well suited to agriculture. In the west a range of mountains runs parallel to the north coast for about a hundred miles. In the centre stretches a further range near the south coast while in the easternmost province of Oriente are Cuba's highest mountains, the legendary Sierra Maestra, historic guerrilla stronghold and base of the Rebel Army.

Although Cuba is on the fringe of the tropics, the climate is pleasantly moderated by the surrounding oceans with an average annual temperature of around 24.6°C rising to about 25°C in summer and falling very slightly in winter. Rarely is it really cold and farmers have no need to fear frost. Most rain falls in the wet season from May to October, but often there is a little rain in most months of the dry season (November to April). Droughts occur often enough to cause serious worry and August, September and October are the months of the hurricanes that can do tremendous damage.

Largest of the West Indies, Cuba is really a narrow,

crocodile-shaped archipelago as can be seen from the map on the endpapers, stretching twelve hundred kilometres from west to east. Her long indented coastline is washed by the warm waters of the Caribbean Sea and dotted with over a thousand islets or keys forming innumerable sheltered bays. Largest of these is the Isle of Pines. But the geographical fact that perhaps more than any other has helped to shape Cuba's destiny is the short distance of a hundred and eighty kilometres, a day's voyage, which separates Cuba from the coast of North America at Key West, Florida.

However, events linked Cuba with the culture of Spanish South America well over a century before the Pilgrim Fathers founded the first of the United States. It was at the beginning of the sixteenth century, seventeen years after the visit of Columbus, that Spain then a nation state with a strongly centralised government, sent an expeditionary force under Diego de Velasquez to search for gold and set to work a native labour force with a view to extracting riches from the new found island of Cuba. Columbus had found its first inhabitants whom he called Indians, a gentle courteous and hospitable people. They were known as the Siboney and the Taino Indians and it is thought that they were races of the Arawak language group some of whom worked flint, made pottery, wove baskets and practised primitive agriculture. They used canoes to fish the coastal waters and for food they grew corn, and such root crops as sweet potatoes, cassava and manioc. They also cultivated tobacco which they rolled into cigars and for shelter they built round huts thatched with palm leaves in which they hung woven hammocks. When news reached them from near-by islands of the exploits of the Spanish plunderers, they organised themselves in small guerrilla type groups under the leadership of Hatuey, a Dominican Indian chief, and prepared to resist. The Spaniards waged battle with armour and horses and ships, gunpowder and dogs and in two years the island was quelled. Then with great vigour the conquerors set about constructing a viable colony only to find that the gold they sought was not forthcoming except in unrewarding quantities.

14

The Spaniards brought with them to Cuba the culture of their homeland – the pattern of their family life, language, religion, political and legal institutions and the Spanish style of architecture that is still a feature of the ancient cities of Cuba today.

The early conquistadors were rewarded for service by gifts of large estates in the island to which clans of Indians were attached as a labour force. This local population was compelled to mine for metals, sift for gold dust in the streams and work for long hours on the land at tasks for which they were totally unfitted. A Spanish Dominican friar, conscience stricken by what he had seen, had the courage to report the sufferings of the Indians to the Spanish homeland and for this he is still honoured in Spanish America today. But the damage was done. While the numbers who survived may have been somewhat underestimated, it is clear that as a race the Indians were virtually exterminated in Cuba. Totally unsuited to the new life, with the structure of their own society broken down, they died in thousands. There were risings harshly suppressed, the last one in 1529, but soon there were very few Indians left to rebel.

The dwindling numbers of Indians raised labour problems for the Spanish settlers, particularly in a tropical climate, and already they had begun to look elsewhere for new sources of labour of greater stamina than the Indians. The winds and currents of the Atlantic took the boats of Spanish traders to the coasts of Africa. Here it was good business to unload goods and pack the empty space with African slave labour. Soon the right to supply Spain's colonies with slaves was much sought after particularly by English traders like Sir John Hawkins who helped to build Britain's wealth on this lucrative trade and in the following centuries Africans were imported to Cuba in large numbers. The census returns for Cuba in 1774 gave the population as 171,000 of which 44,000 were Africans and 31,000 mixed blood. Although marriage between races was discouraged by colonial law, the large number of mixed race is significant – mostly sons and daughters of mixed Spanish and African parenthood. Alejandro de Humboldt, a visitor to Cuba at this time, described Havana as seen from the shore as most gay and picturesque: a small city within its city walls, parks, promenades, convents, churches, tiled wooden houses and sumptuous residences, straight streets filled with cosmopolitan crowds 'where the mixture of colour abounded (*abundo mucho las mexcla de color*)'. This mixture of races has been very evident throughout the centuries and is part of Cuba's rich and varied inheritance.

The structure of Spanish colonial society in the island is often compared to a pyramid. At the peak were the Spanish military authorities and colonial functionaries, followed closely by Cuban-born (Creole) landowners and wealthy merchants – descendants often of the original Spanish settlers. At the base were the African slaves and in between were craftsmen, artisans, poets, artists, musicians and free working people of many races. Just as the white population as divided into those born in Spain and those born in Cuba, so among the 'people of colour' the colonial regime differentiated between Africans born in Africa and those born in Cuba, between slaves and freed slaves and these were further divided according to the shade of colour of their skin into light and dark brown (*pardos y morenos*).

Under the Spanish Code, slaves could in theory buy their freedom. (How to find the money was another question and for women it often meant prostitution.) In Cuba, however, census figures show that there was a large number of free people of African descent long before slavery was abolished. The 1774 census gave 96,440 whites, 31,847 free coloured and 44,333 slaves. Children born to a slave and fathered by a white master were often given their freedom. They and their children then joined the class of free 'people of colour' (blacks and 'pardos') who themselves under Spanish colonial law could and sometimes did own slaves.

A prize-winning study of Havana in the years 1820-1845, *The Negro in the Economy of Havana in the Nineteenth Century* by the Cuban writer Pedro Deschamps Chapeaux (Havana

1971) shows that, while many free black people lived along with poor whites in extreme poverty, by great perseverance some were able to overcome the barriers of a hierarchical society and play a significant part in the economy of Cuba. The author describes the importance of the *cabildo* in preserving African culture in Cuban society. The cabildo was an African religious and mutual aid society through which each main tribal group owned its own headquarters, elected a governing council of men and women according to tribal custom and, as well as providing a community centre for dance and music in its own national traditions, generally looked after the affairs of its people.

Legal documents of the 1820-45 period provide numerous examples of free citizens of Havana of African descent who had established themselves successfully in certain trades and professions. As artists and musicians, fashionable tailors and hairdressers, shoemakers and mechanics, midwives and teachers a section of the urban black population of both sexes formed at this time an important and, in some cases, thriving property-owning part of Havana's economy. Some had also received military training in the Battalions of Loyal Blacks and Mulattos, Negro regiments formed in the seventeenth century for service in Spain's colonial wars.

Trouble came, however, when Negroes began to qualify as surgeons and dentists and to enter trades usually the preserve of white people. This was seen by the authorities as a threat to the established order of society and greatly feared accordingly. In 1843 and the following year the Spanish General Military Command was sent to crush slave uprisings in the sugar mills of Matanzas. These revolts took place against impossible odds for not only was the Spanish army concentrated here in the west of Cuba, but here too the slave system was strongest and the Cuban landowners in greatest fear of the abolition of slavery. In 1844, the authorities claimed to have uncovered a widespread conspiracy for the abolition of slavery and a free Cuba, the so-called Conspiración de la Escalera. This was a signal for terrible retribution. The black regiments were disbanded as a precaution and penal measures were taken particularly against free blacks who had begun to rise in society. A commission sentenced seventy-eight to death, twelve hundred and ninety-two to prison, four hundred to exile and many hundreds died under the lash so that the year 1844 went down in history as the Year of the Lash. As well as the many slaves who perished, the result was to wipe out the rising middle classes of the free Negroes and their best leaders as well as many liberal whites who were opposed to slavery. The wars of independence of the next century began in the eastern regions of the island where slavery had least hold on the economic and social life and in these wars where white and black fought side by side, the free black population formed a large proportion of those who took up arms and gave their lives for Cuba to become a free nation.

Farming traditions in Cuba

Cuba's importance to Spain in the beginning was as a base for trade and the defence of her American colonies. Havana then as now was a beautiful natural harbour strategically placed on important sea routes. Fleets of treasure ships sailing in convoy and laden with bullion from the mines of Mexico and Peru, stopped at the harbour for supplies, then made use of the gulf stream to sail swiftly to Spain. The port became Spain's main naval base and Havana began to acquire those characteristics which led historians to describe her as 'already a centre of vice, gambling, crime and prostitution'.

Outside Havana, in the countryside of the interior, livestock raising was at first Cuba's main industry. Semi-wild herds first imported by the early Spanish settlers, roamed at will over large circular estates. These were owned in common by groups of ranchers who shared the profits from the sale of hides, tallow and dried meat. This land pattern began to change in the seventeenth century with the appearance of cultivated fields of tobacco and sugar in increasing numbers. Both crops were well suited to Cuba's soil and climate.

Tobacco, Cuba's oldest industry, was also for a long time its largest industry. In the middle of the nineteenth century about half of the population depended in some way on tobacco for a living. The plant is native to Cuba and has for centuries been grown on various sized farms throughout the island, Pinar del Rio and Las Villas being the great tobacco growing areas. There are two methods of cultivation and in the photograph on Plate XV shade tobacco can be seen growing under canopies of cheese cloth stretched on poles. This shade tobacco has a lighter leaf than sun tobacco which is grown in the open fields. The leaves are picked and dried usually in airy drying sheds, and certain kinds are rolled to make the famous Havana cigars. After the abolition of slavery and the massive investment of American capital at the end of the nineteenth century, tobacco developed into Cuba's first large scale industry with many small farmers losing ownership of their land to large companies and becoming either wage earners or, for the most part, share croppers. In the latter case, the company owned the land and house, often advancing money for which a high price had to be paid. The farmer then provided labour and, often, oxen and equipment, and received a share of the profits.

Militant action in tobacco communities took place as early as 1717-23 in risings against the tobacco monopoly while some of Cuba's first craft guilds were formed by the skilled men of the industry – tobacco sorters and selectors, master cigar makers and decorators. The strongly knit communities in which tobacco workers lived tended, as in British mining communities, to encourage solidarity and these became strongholds of the early trade unionism, with an emphasis on worker's education and a tradition of commissioning readers to read aloud. With the concentration of workers into large factories, the tobacco industry also became the centre of the new national trade union movement and produced some of its outstanding leaders. One of their number was Lazara Peña, until his recent death secretary of the Confederation of Cuban Trade Unions.

Good soil, a warm climate and moisture are needed for

growing sugar cane and in most years Cuba can supply all these. The sweet juice is contained in the stem of the plant and to maintain the quantity and quality of the juice, planting must be repeated every other year or so and the cane processed immediately it is cut. At the time of the *zafra* when the sugar is harvested and brought to the mills, thousands of field workers arm themselves with the traditional all purpose knife – the machete – and cut down the cane at ground level, trim off the leaves and stack the stalks into carts or trucks to be carried to the mills. By the end of the seventeenth century, the sugar industry was based on about one hundred small mills owned by white colonists and at first showed no sign of that rapid growth that was to earn Cuba the name of 'the sugar bowl of Europe'. By 1860, the number of sugar mills had risen to about two thousand.

The *cafetal* or coffee plantation was another historic type of Cuban farming. The coffee bush is a shade-loving plant and is grown in the mountains often in the shadow of banana and other shade trees. On the large plantations as many as a hundred slaves were sometimes used. Here the farmers would own their own mills for removing the hulls from the coffee beans, and grow rice and vegetables for their own needs. But coffee was also grown on many small farms often on rented land.

Increasingly the wealthy classes of Europe acquired a taste for Cuba's excellent cigars, coffee and sugar and later a weakened Spain was in no position to prevent Cuba trading with others besides herself. During the first half of the eighteenth century, more and more land was broken up to meet the demand and forests of valuable timber were cut down to feed the mills. Internally, too, the demand grew for maize, fruit, root vegetables and other crops to feed the great influx of slaves and the bigger number of work animals now used. Cuba became one of Spain's most valuable colonies.

It was in 1762 that Great Britain, Spain's enemy in the Seven Year's War, sent a powerful armada which captured Havana after a siege of forty days and established English rule for nearly a year. Cubans today look on this period as one which opened up new horizons in free trade putting the island in touch with the world. It also led to certain improvements in civil liberties which had their effect even when the island was returned to Spanish administration.

Effects of the French and American Revolutions

Cuba felt the impact of the French and American revolutions and the rise of the European bourgeoisie both on ideas and on the economy. For the island the years 1790-1839 were times of considerable commercial and intellectual awakening. Prosperity following upon broader international trade brought more leisure for the Cuban middle classes which in its turn stimulated literature and the arts and about this time the Academy of Literature was founded. Partly because of her position as an international port, news of scientific inventions and discoveries quickly found their way to Havana. The steam engine invented by Watt in 1792 functioned in Havana in 1796 and Cuba became the fourth in the world to establish a railway. Mass vaccination against smallpox was pioneered in Havana and in 1855 the island had its first experience of electric light. Young philosophers like Father Félix Varela (1788-1853) and historians like José Antonio Saco (1797-1879) were keen to open up Cuba to modern ideas and this new spirit of enquiry was reflected in a desire to see her free from the stifling bonds of the old colonial society. Cultural associations flourished and there was much interest in creating a new, more scientific education. One famous educationalist, Joseda la Luz y Caballero, wrote to a friend: 'Everything here is full of enthusiasm . . . so return quickly my friend and bring with you books, paintings, rocks and everything for our Ateneo [Association]. This is our motto. Let us unite our efforts, let us improve our culture. Let us build a Fatherland.'

The commerce that widened horizons at the end of the eighteenth century also brought a boom in the slave trade which greatly increased the proportion of the population in

Cuba who in order to live had to work for others. In the forty years from 1790-1830 227,000 African slaves arrived in Cuba nearly doubling the population in that period. From 1791-1868 the total population increased from 272,000 to 1,350,000.

When in 1791, the slaves of the neighbouring colony of Haiti took power and drove out the French sugar barons, Cuba reaped the harvest of Haiti's lost sugar exports and sugar prices rocketed. Cuban coffee also benefited because many French planters left Haiti and transferred their farms and their culture to Cuba. At the same time the wealthy white Cuban landowners who depended on slaves to produce their wealth took fright at what had happened in Haiti. The result was that when the other Latin American colonies rose against Spain in 1810-1820, 'the ever faithful isle' as the Spanish kings called Cuba, did not revolt, partly because Cuba's landed classes feared that her slave population might use the opportunity to seize their own freedom. Thus slavery for a time became a barrier to separation from Spain. Nevertheless even while Napoleon was invading Spain, groups of Cubans were already conspiring for Cuba's independence. It was a time when numerous Cuban families were firmly rooted on middle-sized estates which flourished under their personal direction. The majority were themselves descendents of the Spanish colonists but gradually over the centuries some of them had been developing into a social class which chafed under the restrictions imposed by Spain and, wanting to play a bigger role in their country, began to yearn for political autonomy.

Meanwhile on Cuba's doorstep a new nation was growing and expanding at a rapid rate. England's former American colonies had won their war of independence and now as the United States of America represented a powerful economic force looking around for room to expand in a world already divided up between older empire builders. The States had long shown great interest in Cuba's raw products, especially unrefined sugar. Little by little, despite costly restrictions imposed by Spain, trade which flowed between Cuba and the mother country began to flow in the direction of the United States. By the middle of the nineteenth century, the United States was taking forty per cent of Cuba's exports compared with twelve per cent going to Spain.

One reason for this arose from an event in Europe that hit Cuba hardest in the place where it hurt most: her sugar industry. When wars and blockades brought the threat of starvation to France and England, their governments decided to encourage sugar beet growers by giving their crop a subsidy. As a result Europe was soon growing enough sugar to satisfy most of the home demand. Sugar beet competition proved too great for Cuba's cane. Prices slumped and brought a series of crises in 1847, '57 and '67 which spelt great misery for sugar workers and bad times for Cuba.

The 1868 rising and the Ten Years' War

The feeling was fairly widespread among Cuban land-owners at this time that the only hope of obtaining prosperity and freedom from Spain without disturbing the slave-owning basis of the economy lay with the annexation of Cuba by the United States of America. However, when General Narciso López, backed by Cubans and Americans in the United States, landed with a force of six hundred men in the hope of causing a general uprising in support of annexation, there was insufficient support. The feelings of the majority of Cubans was expressed by Saco, the writer and patriot, when he wrote in 1848: 'I would like to see Cuba not only rich, illustrious, moral and powerful but also not Anglo-American. One day Cuba, our beloved Cuba, will be Cuba.'

The movement for total freedom from Spain grew rapidly and included the most forward-looking of Cuba's farming community. These farmers owned lands throughout the island, a fact that helped to create a truly national consciousness as secret *Free Cuba* societies spread to every region.

23

In 1868, revolt against Spanish domination burst into open rebellion. The signal for the uprising came from the eastern province of Oriente where the movement was strongest and where there was a considerable peasant population with the least reliance on slave labour. Cuban records recall the historic moment when about a hundred patriots under the leadership of Carlos Manuel de Céspedes, a plantation owner of the region, entered the town of Yara near Bayamo and raised the cry of 'Free Cuba. Independence or death.' And here in the mountains of the east, Cubans took to guerrilla warfare as they were to do again and again in the next hundred years. Céspedes, Father of the Wars of Independence as he was later to be known, describes in a letter to the U.S. ambassador to Cuba, Sumner Wells, why the war was of necessity a people's war of a guerrilla type. He writes: 'Because of the configuration and the topography of the land, depopulated and with tremendous forests, and being as it is the struggle of an entire people with its diverse social classes against the oppressing power, abundant in the resources which the former lack,' the struggle could take no other form.

The young Cuban bourgeoisie needed the support of black as well as white and declared as one of the aims of the war the abolition of slavery. Progressive landowners already interested in ideas reaching them from abroad concerning new mechanical inventions came to realise that modern ways of farming could best be achieved by the liberation of their slaves and their transformation into wage earners. On practical as well as on moral grounds they joined their workers in wishing to see the end of slavery. Carlos Manuel de Céspedes, a man of strongly republican and abolitionist sentiments, set an example by freeing his own slaves and promising freedom to whoever volunteered to fight. Many Africans joined the rebel soldiery and Antonio Maceo, national hero and general of outstanding bravery, was himself of African descent. Armed often only with a sword-like knife, the guerrilla bands went into the attack, controlling for a time a large area in the east which was declared the Republic of Free Cuba.

During this ferocious war in which the Cubans were greatly outnumbered by the conventional Spanish Army, 80,000 Spaniards and 400,000 Cubans are said to have been killed while vast areas of sugar fields and half the sugar mills were destroyed. When the uneasy peace was made in 1878, gradual emancipation of slaves was promised. (Complete abolition did not come until 1886, less than one hundred years ago.)

José Martí 1853-1895

Since the main demands of the rebellion had not been achieved General Antonio Maceo refused to sign what he saw as a betrayal. a treaty for peace without independence for Cuba. Forced to leave the country, he began to make preparations for further struggle. With him in this task was José Martí, founder of the Revolutionary Party of Cuba, poet and soldier whose writings and revolutionary example inspired generations of Cubans. Son of a Spaniard who had served in the Spanish army, he was only fifteen when the Ten Years War started and at seventeen he was condemned to six years hard labour and exile for his part in a demonstration calling for Cuba's independence. When the war ended, as a young man in his mid-twenties, he devoted his energies to building the Revolutionary Party which, when it was formed in 1872, included representatives of workers' clubs among whom was the Marxist Carlos Balino, co-founder fifty-three years later of the Cuban Communist Party. It was while José Martí was writing in the United States that he warned of the danger to the South American continent of interference and financial penetration by their powerful neighbour – 'the Colossus of the North' as he called her. He stressed the common interests and culture of Latin American countries and urged their people to stand on their own feet and so achieve a dignified freedom without substituting one master for another.

25

José Martí must have been well aware of the rapid investment of North American capital in Cuba at this time, particularly in the sugar industry. During the ten years of fighting, the destruction by fire of vast areas meant that many old mills were either totally destroyed or in drastic need of repair. Many Cuban mill owners were unable to raise the capital and American business interests stepped in. By the end of the nineteenth century, foreign capital was invested in Cuba in a big way. With steel becoming cheaper around 1880, railways built with United States capital replaced the slow oxen which carried sugar cane to the mills. This meant that the large steam driven mills could process greater quantities of sugar cane. To gain more land wealthy mill owners, often foreign companies, bought out the small landowners and the trend began to the concentration of land ownership into sugar *latisfundia* – the huge sugar concerns of the twentieth century.

Thus both the influx of foreign capital into large scale industry and the abolition of slavery led to a big increase in the size of Cuba's working class. By 1890 and throughout the twentieth century, an increasing number of white Cubans were working on the sugar plantations. Many Spanish immigrants originally came to Cuba to set up business but when these failed their descendents became wage earners. Some went into the sugar industry and along with black Cubans and immigrant West Indian workers, they shared the central hardship of all sugar workers: the fact that sugar only provided steady jobs in most cases for a few months of the year. The harvest sugar-making season kept men working at great intensity from January to June. Then came what was known as the *dead season* for the rest of the year. Right until 1959 it was accepted as a fact of Cuban life that a third of the industrial workers were employed for less than six months annually with no unemployment relief while in some years thousands of agricultural wage earners averaged only four months work. Hence even in times of prosperity there was a sharp contrast between sections of extreme poverty and a comparatively rich land.

Through eight years of uneasy peace José Martí and his Revolutionary Party, together with generals Maximo Gomez, Calixto Garcia and Antonio Maceo, had been preparing the people for the final struggle against Spain. 1868 had proved to the Cubans that, inspired by the cause of Free Cuba, they could stand up effectively to the Spanish Army even though outnumbered and poorly armed. Now they were better equipped and could go into the fight on more equal terms. Moreover, the writings of Martí had aroused national consciousness to a pitch where an increasing number of Cubans were prepared to risk death for a free Cuba because they believed with him that 'He who loves the homeland cannot think of himself.' Martí based himself on the underprivileged but his genius in uniting people of varying beliefs won the support of the majority of Cubans, including those living abroad, in what was to be the final fight for independence from Spain in 1895-1898.

'You take your rights,' he had written, 'you do not beg for them: you do not buy them with tears but blood.' Soon after the war started, in 1895, he himself forfeited his life when he was killed fighting with the guerrillas after he had landed on the eastern shores of Cuba. The influence of José Martí was great during his lifetime but his philosophy was to have even more far reaching influence in our own age.

Cuba's War of Independence lasted three years. Under the outstanding leadership of General Gomez and especially the legendary Antonio Maceo, 'the bronze Titan', the Cuban rebels, although still outnumbered, broke through all attempts to confine the war to the east. In an effort to contain the war, the Spanish military authorities removed the rural populations, largely women and children from the east into camps near the cities of the west. Here with practically total lack of food and sanitation they died in hundreds of thousands. So many small children under the age of four died in these three years that their age group is strikingly small on all future population tables. Martinez Ortiz, the

Cuban historian who was thirty years of age at the time, describes the dereliction of great stretches of the countryside where every trace of husbandry had been annihilated and the consequent abysmal condition of the working people. He estimates the cost of the war as 400,000 lives.

There is one man still living in Cuba at the time of writing who has lived through the struggles of the last hundred years and given his personal view of them. He heard the echoes of the 1868 uprising from the mountain forests where, as a runaway slave, he was in hiding. When the Ten Years War was over and slavery partially abolished, he returned to life and work on a sugar plantation. Later in 1895 he joined as a soldier in Cuba's War of Independence and fought under Antonio Maceo. He is Esteban Montejo and he was a hundred and three in 1963 when he told his memories to Miguel Barnet, anthropologist, who wrote them down as they were spoken and later published them in biographical form.

There used to be a saying in Cuba. no sugar – no country. Certainly the very existence of Esteban Montejo was geared to the production of sugar. He explains that he was one of thousands of African babies who were bred like cattle on the plantations to supply labour for the sugar fields and the sugar mills. One of his first jobs in sugar making was to lead a mule and wagon piled high with *bagasse* – the fibre left after the juices have been extracted from the sugar cane. This was unloaded at the sugar mill town where the mill workers lived. There it was spread out to dry and taken later to the furnaces to be used as fuel. Youngsters on this job grew hunchbacked from bearing down on the hard mouthed mules. He describes the large dwelling places called *barracoons* where he lived on the plantation.

'Around two hundred slaves of all colours lived in the Flor de Sagua barracoon. It was laid out in rows. two rows facing each other with a door in the middle and a massive padlock to shut the slaves in at night. For ventilation there was just a hole in the wall or a barred window, with the result that the place swarmed with flies and ticks which made the inmates ill . . . The salvation of the slaves were the little strips of land where they grew sweet potatoes, gourds, kidney beans, yucca and peanuts . . . Life was hard and bodies wore out . . . I saw many horrors as punishment under slavery. That was why I didn't like the life.' So Esteban decided to make a break for the forest and there he remained until news reached him that slaves were to be freed. Later he gives an ordinary soldier's view of the 1895 war and its causes when at the age of thirty-five, with thousands of others, he took up his machete, borrowed a horse from a farmer and offered his services: 'What all of us wanted as Cubans was the freedom of Cuba. We wanted the Spaniards to go and leave us alone. "Freedom or death" people said or "Free Cuba".' Later he explains:

'I myself know that war destroys men's trust, your brothers die beside you and there is nothing you can do about it. Then along come the smart guys and grab all the good jobs . . . Nevertheless the war was needed. It was all wrong that so many jobs and privileges should fall into the hands of the Spaniards and women should have to sleep with Spaniards to get work. None of this was right. You never saw a Negro lawyer, because they said Negroes were not good for anything except the forest. It was all kept for the white Spaniards. Even the white Creoles (Cuban born) were pushed aside. I saw this happen. A watchman with nothing to do except walk up and down, call the hour and put out the light had to be a Spaniard. It was the same everywhere. There was no freedom. I realised this when the leaders explained it all to us. That is why we had to go to war.'

While the Cubans were fighting their own successful but still undecided war, the Americans intervened.

With their shores only ninety miles away from Cuba, Americans were understandably following every phase of the fighting. Pressure for intervention was great and motives were mixed. Many American citizens, horrified by tales of the ferocity of the war, wanted intervention for humanitarian reasons to stop the slaughter. Others wanted the

Cubans to win their independence as they had won theirs. But the overriding political reason was frankly stated in the debate that followed a mysterious explosion on the *U.S.S. Maine* in February 1898 while she was in harbour at Havana. During the debate, speakers repeatedly declared that it was the destiny of the United States to control Cuba. In doing so they were repeating the sentiments of Senator Stephen A. Douglas speaking in New Orleans twenty years before. 'It is our destiny to have Cuba and it is folly to debate the question.'

Finally, after considerable hesitation, U.S. President Kinley in his message to United States Congress stated that intervention as a neutral in the Cuban-Spanish war was justified 'by the serious injury to commerce, trade and business of our people and by the wanton destruction of property and devastation of the island.' (By 1896 Americans owned thirty million dollars worth of sugar properties and by the same year America had invested fifteen million dollars in mining properties and five million in tobacco, so there was much United States property at risk in Cuba).

The day before the President's message to Congress he received a note from the American minister in Madrid advising that it had been indicated to him that immediate peace could be obtained from Spain by negotiation either on the basis of independence or by ceding the island to the United States. However, only a passing reference was made to the communication and on April 19th 1898, the United States declared war on Spain. In a few months the war was over and on December 10th 1898, a peace treaty was signed in Paris and by January 1st 1899, Spanish troops had left the island for ever.

The peace treaty recognised the independence of Cuba and provided for the protection of private property and pacification of Cuba by the United States and to this end General Wood took over as military Governor of Cuba.

When the United States Congress decided to intervene in the Spanish–Cuban war, the resolution calling upon Spain to withdraw her forces and revoke her sovereignty also

30

contained the following clause:

'The United States hereby disclaims any disposition or intent to exercise authority, jurisdiction or control over the said island except for the pacification thereof, and asserts its determination when that is accomplished to leave government and control of the island to its people.'

Two years later the same Congress passed into law a set of articles which it insisted should be included in the new constitution of Cuba before the occupation army was withdrawn. These articles were known as the Platt Amendment. Among other things, they gave the United States 'the right to intervene for the preservation of Cuban independence the maintenance of a Government adequate for the protection of life, property and individual liberty.' They also provided for the Cuban Government to sell or lease agreed land to the United States for a coaling, naval and defence base. (This base exists to this day.)

While the amendment was finally added to the constitution by a small majority vote, the Cubans protested that the promise of independence meant being independent 'of every other nation, the great and noble American nation included', for they feared that these articles would be used as a restriction of their sovereignty. The history of the twentieth century shows how far their fears were justified.

Meanwhile let Esteban Montejo give a revolutionary soldier's impressions of the end of the war and the end of an epoch. Outspoken and controversial as ever, he describes to his biographer both the immediate joy of victory and the disillusion at its results:

'I felt happy,' he tells. 'I never believed the war could end. It was like when I had been in the forest and heard that slavery had been abolished ... When they told me an armistice had been declared, I took no notice. But Havana convinced me completely. The whole town seemed to have gone crazy with joy. The people cheered Maximo Gomez in the streets and kissed his jacket. There wasn't a Cuban that didn't go round shouting "Long live Cuba".

'The people of Havana seemed to think the Americans

were coming there for fun, but then they realised their mistake, and that all they wanted was the biggest slice of the cake. The mass of the people just sat back and let it happen. There were even some people who rejoiced that the Americans had taken the initiative.'

Speaking of American intervention at Santiago de Cuba where the Spanish army surrendered, he says: 'The Americans bombarded the place, but it was Calixto García who attacked Vara el Ray's men by land and destroyed them. Then the Americans ran up their flag to show they had taken the city. The worst thing was that the commanding officer ordered that no Cubans should enter the city. That was what made everyone's blood boil. When the Cubans found they were not allowed in they began to resent the Americans.'

He concludes: 'The Americans wheedled their way into possession of Cuba but they don't really deserve all the blame. It was the Cubans who obeyed them who were the really guilty ones.'

THE RISE AND FALL OF A REPUBLIC

WHEN AMERICA intervened in Cuba's war against Spain, she
was a young dynamic capitalist state pursuing commercial
expansion at a time when big trading companies were
beginning to operate on a national and international scale.
Her outlook at this period was well expressed by a Senator
Albert J. Beveridge. Speaking in Washington two days before
war was declared on Spain, he said: 'American factories are
making more than American people can use. American soil
is producing more than they can consume. Fate has written
our policy for us: the trade of the world must and shall be
ours. And we will get it as our mother England has shown us
how. We will establish trading posts throughout the world as
distributing points for American products. We will cover the
oceans with our merchant marine. We will build up a navy
to the measure of our greatness. Great colonies governing
themselves but flying our flag and trading with us, will grow
about our posts of trade. Our institutions will follow our flag
on the wings of commerce. And American law, American
order, American civilisation will plant themselves on shores
hitherto blooded and benighted, but by these agencies of
God henceforth to be made bright and beautiful.'

When the American military Governor and his troops
departed from the shores of Cuba, he had endeavoured to
leave them more bright and beautiful by building roads and
introducing an elementary school system on the American
pattern, and in 1902 Cuba was declared a republic. But
basically her political independence remained severely
limited by the terms of the controversial Platt Amendment
which formed part of the Cuban constitution for three
decades. During these years the island was governed by
politicians supported by the United States one of whose

33

ambassadors once described his office as that of 'the most important man in Cuba, sometimes more important than the Cuban president'. Three times in 1906, 1912 and 1917, Congress took the step of sending troops to Cuba to intervene against popular unrest.

When the defeated Spaniards fled after the wars of independence, their estates were bought up cheaply by foreign companies and banks and the old caste pattern of Cuban life was shattered for ever as a host of speculators and waves of immigrants converged on the island from all parts of the world. Cuban sugar received specially favourable prices in America in return for tariff-reduction on United States goods sold in Cuba. As a result trade with England, Spain, France, Germany and other countries, which was quite considerable in the early years of the century, after the First World War was largely replaced by an import-export trade developed round a single customer – the United States. In 1905–22 Cuba got 47% of her imports from the U.S., in 1923–27 65% and by 1938–39 67.5%.

There was rapid development in the first years of the republic. New towns arose with exclusive suburbs and gradually the soaring outlines of fine public buildings and elegant hotels began to change the skyline of the old Havana. (Later Cuba's telephone system was to rival North America's and when private motor cars arrived on the scene, Havana had more per head of population than many a major city.) All this was a reflection of the spectacular way in which Cuba's raw sugar production began to swell in the early years of the republic with good effect on the island's balance of payments. More and more land was put down to cane and a network of railways carried cane to the new centrals – great mills like factories in the field employing up to two thousand workers. Between 1901 and 1920 in Cuba's sugar gold rush, the harvest increased from just over a million to four million tons.

Cuban business men shared in the new prosperity but in the long run a national industry could not compete with cheap imports and large-scale foreign-owned enterprises, many of them branches of U.S. firms which shipped their profits back to the home country. A World Bank Report on Cuba (1951) shows that with all the new investment little encouragement was given to creating a varied local industry. In a land where soil and climate are near perfect for fruit growing, the report states that of eleven million kilos of tomatoes exported annually, nine million returned to Cuba as tomato sauce, paste and ketchup and although processing was the most profitable part of the meat industry, none of Cuba's meat products were processed in Cuba at that time. This lop-sided growth meant that while big investors were making quick profits, disease, poverty, and seasonal unemployment remained widespread particularly in the countryside thus increasing the contrasts between rich and poor and tending to heighten the contradictions in Cuban society.

In the 'twenties the price of sugar rocketed, creating millionaires overnight and resulting in a spending spree that earned the name 'dance of the millions'. The boom, however, was short lived. Overproduction throughout the world brought sugar prices down sharply and since Cuba's economy was largely geared to sugar, wide spread ruin resulted. Once more Cuban-owned mills and Cuban banks went bankrupt and once more Cuban farms were bought by foreign capital. Large numbers of independent tobacco and sugar growers lost their farms in the crisis, many of them moving away from their own province to work as wage earners or join the pool of unemployed.

The generation of the 'thirties

The world crisis of the 'twenties hit the Cuban workers particularly hard. It also had a profound effect on the young people of Cuba, particularly the first republican-born generation who came of age in the 'twenties full of disillusion with the results of independence. One of them, a Cuban writer Luis E. Aguilar who has since left Cuba, recalls the winds of change sweeping through Latin America in the nineteen-twenties and 'thirties and describes how 'the vibrating thunder of the Russian Revolution although remote and obscure attracted the attention of workers'. Communist Parties and radical groups appeared in several countries and Cuba was no exception. During this period Cuban trade unionism took a powerful step forward with the formation of the National Confederation of Cuban Workers. University students, too, formed their own Students Union (FEU) in the mid-twenties and won the respect of the workers by their vigorous support in wage struggles.

Typical of the new rebellious spirit among left-wing intellectuals was one incident in particular. At a time when gangsterism and corruption was as notorious in Cuban governing circles as the Watergate revelations have become in our own day, the Minister of Justice was invited as chief guest at a dinner-meeting of the Academy of Science. In protest at the corruption of the Ministry of which the Minister was a representative, thirteen prominent Cuban intellectuals led by a young communist poet Rubén Martínez Villena walked out of the meeting and later published a statement giving their reasons. Newspapers gave the incident full publicity and the 'Protest of the Thirteen' became a rallying call to the nation not to remain silent.

In 1925, Gerardo Machado, sometimes known by Cubans as the tropical Mussolini, became president in one of the stormiest periods of Cuban history. At first he enjoyed personal popularity and there was high hope that he would carry out promises to develop Cuban industry and in his own phrase 'achieve political independence through economic independence'. He did in fact raise tariffs to protect Cuban fruits, rice, cocoa and textiles but before long he had also introduced a law that gave American-controlled electricity and transport companies the right to expropriate from the Cuban state and from private individuals all the land and property they needed for expanding services. As the general crisis deepened, Machado clung to personal power at all costs and met violent unrest among workers and students by open dictatorship. While soldiers paraded in the streets of Cuba's main cities, he banned political meetings and closed universities. (The universities remained closed for three years.) Among workers' leaders deported, imprisoned or assassinated were many Spanish anarchists, some of the earliest pioneers of socialist ideas in Cuba.

Despite increasing repression, the strike movement continued to spread culminating in a national day of action against unemployment on March 20th 1930, with hunger marches throughout Latin America and a twenty-four-hour general strike in Cuba of 200,000 workers. This was accompanied by a crescendo of student protest ending in a violent demonstration in September of the same year in which a student Rafael Trejo died in clashes with the police.

One of Cuba's outstanding national heroes of this period was the student leader Julio Antonio Mella, joint founder of the old Cuban Communist Party. He strove for student-worker unity and was the inspiration behind the formation of a People's University where both could exchange knowledge and experience. He was imprisoned, went on hunger strike and was later deported to Mexico where he was killed, it was thought by Machado's assassins.

1933 – a landmark in Cuban history with almost half the active population unemployed – saw a second general strike initiated by the sugar workers transformed into a nation-wide uprising against Machado's regime. Cuba's eight-year-old Communist Party was particularly strong among the sugar central workers who were spread throughout the country and in touch with miners, railwaymen, farm labourers, nickel refinery and other rural workers. Leaders of the unions were mainly left wing and among them were many communists but the depth of the revolt took even these leaders by surprise as busmen, textile workers and others refused to return to work although all their demands had been met. Popular anger reached boiling point when machine guns were turned on the crowds who had first been decoyed into the streets by an officially circulated false rumour that General Machado had agreed to retire. The workers seized and occupied several railway terminals and ports and, in thirty sugar-mill towns, the sugar workers established short lived local soviets, workers councils after the Russian style. Faced by open insurrection and abandoned even by his army, Machado was overthrown as the people wreaked bloody vengeance on his collaborators in the streets.

Fidel Castro was only a boy of six or seven at the time but later he and the July 26th Movement were to trace their roots to the generation of the 'thirties. Their manifesto stated: 'Of that generation of the 'thirties despite its romantic immaturity . . . in the hundred days that the revolutionary forces held power, they did more in the defence of the interests of the nation than all the governments of the preceding years.'

For a brief hundred days in 1933 a government backed by students and a section of the army, and composed mainly of young people, held office under Ramón Grau San Martin, a university professor and, as founder of the Authentic Revolutionary Party, opposed to communism. His second in command was Antonio Guiteras Holmes, a left-wing ex-student and exponent of direct action, who was later assassinated. Under his vigorous leadership the group of young people swiftly passed some enlightened legislation including the eight hour day and a minimum wage for canecutters. When this was followed by more radical measures of nationalisation and a call for the end to the Platt Amendment, the American ambassador, who had previously put pressure on Machado to resign in view of mounting public unrest, now became even more alarmed and called on his government to intervene. His demand was not met, but by way of warning U.S. battleships were stationed in the main ports of Cuba. The Grau-Guiteras government never received United States recognition but this was only one of a combination of factors that forced its resignation on January 15 1934.

Twenty years later, Fidel Castro was to draw a lesson from this time when on January 8th 1959 he appealed to student leaders: 'Can you have forgotten what happened after Machado's fall in 1935? One of the greatest ills to attack the revolutionary forces was the proliferation of groups squabbling among themselves. And what happened as a result? Batista came to power and remained there for eleven years.'

The rise of Batista

Fulgencio Batista, an army sergeant of mixed race who led a successful coup against superior officers in the early 'thirties, at first used his popularity in the army to combine with students in setting up the Grau-Guiteras administration. However, when the United States indicated its disapproval by withholding recognition, Batista began to put out feelers in his own interest. He found that the U.S. Congress, worried about its property in Cuba, was prepared to repeal the Platt Amendment and increase the sugar quota in return for a more stable government. Secure in the knowledge of American support and having already used the army against strikers, Batista used his army support to bring down the government he had helped to create and replaced it by an administration dependent on him for its existence. Against the background of the Second World War and its aftermath the cold war, the twists and turns of Batista's path to personal power appear to dominate the surface of the Cuban scene over the next twenty years. Beneath the surface forces were maturing in the wage struggles of the workers, the unrest of the students and the unfulfilled expectations of Cuban small farmers which would finally shake Batista from power together with the political system which produced him.

In the Second World War, Cuba supported Roosevelt and the allies, and in 1942 declared war on Germany, Japan and Italy. During this period Batista took his cue from the Roosevelt administration. At home he sought approval from the workers by supporting progressive measures to improve working conditions and strengthen national industry and in 1939 he formed a coalition of a popular front type in which

39

communists took part. It was the left wing of this coalition that steered through the Constituent Assembly the very enlightened *Constitution of 1940* which, even though for the most part it was not put into practice, by its very existence provided a standard for the future.

A few weeks after the adoption of the constitution, Batista was elected President and later formed a government of national unity. In 1944 he handed over the presidency to Grau San Martin (by now a pillar of the establishment) after elections in which Grau's party, the Autenticos, had been successful. Then Batista retired to Florida there to invest his spoils of office.

On March 10th 1952, ten weeks after popular support had placed a new radical Cuban People's Party top of the opinion polls with its slogan of 'Honesty Before Money', Batista returned to Cuba and, with the help of a small group of officers, suspended the 1940 Constitution and dissolved the political parties. He then proceeded to rule with a degree of bribery and violence rare even in Cuba. Arthur Schlesinger Junior, White House assistant to President Kennedy later, had this to say about Batista's regime in Cuba. 'The rapacity of the leadership, the corruption of the Government, the brutality of the police, the regime's indifference to the needs of the people . . . all these in Cuba as elsewhere, constituted an open invitation to revolution.'

Nine months before Batista's coup, Eduardo Chibás, founder of the Cuban People's Party, shot himself during one of his weekly political broadcasts. To Cubans listening, he addressed his last words. 'People of Cuba awake! This is my last warning!'

Fidel Castro and a new Cuban generation

'This movement is a new Cuban generation with its own ideas, rising up against tyranny made up of young men and women who were barely seven years old when Batista perpetrated the first of his crimes in 1934.' *26th July Movement Manifesto.*

One of the young men to be profoundly affected by the death of Eduardo Chibás, was the young lawyer Fidel Castro y Ruz who had joined his People's Party in 1947 at the age of twenty. His immediate reaction to Batista's seizure of power was to challenge him personally by delivering to the lawcourts two briefs demanding that 'the traitor Batista' be put on trial for criminally overturning the constitution and for high treason.

As a child Fidel Castro lived on his father's sugar plantation in the mountains near Biran on the north coast of Oriente. These mountains have meant much to him all his life and to them and their peasant people he returned during the days of guerrilla war. His father Angel Castro y Argiz came from Spain, as an immigrant farm labourer, to settle in Cuba where he gradually built up a fairly large sugar plantation. His mother, Lina Ruz Gonzalez, was born in Cuba though her parents also came from Galicia.

In one of Fidel Castro's rare reminiscences about his childhood he recalled how when he was about six or seven he told his father he wanted to go to school. Since as a boy he himself had never had the opportunity, his father could not see the necessity and refused. At this the young Fidel declared he would burn the house down if they did not send him to school. Finally he got his way and was packed off to stay with godparents in Santiago de Cuba where he was able to attend the local Jesuit church school. From here in 1942 at the age of sixteen he was sent to the famous Jesuit Higher or Pre-University school called the *Colegio Belen.*

In 1945 at the age of nineteen, Fidel Castro began studying law at Havana University at a time when university life was riddled with the violence prevalent in society as a whole. The degree of that violence was conveyed in a Cuban newspaper account of 1948 which showed that in the four previous years there had been sixty-four political assassinations, thirty-four people wounded by action groups, over two dozen individuals kidnapped and over a hundred assassination attempts. An editorial of a moderate newspaper described the student scene thus: 'Violence holds sway in the

41

halls of the University. Professors and students are nothing but prisoners of a few groups of student gangsters who impose their will at gunpoint. The University Council has declared its inability to remove these gangs . . .'

Havana University had long been one of the main power centres in Cuban politics but the political action groups of the 'thirties seem to have degenerated by the middle nineteen forties into rival gangs mainly concerned with running black market and protection rackets. Fidel Castro told students of the university during a visit in 1959 that his student days were among the most dangerous of his life with at least one attempt on his life. After his first year, he seems to have thrown in his lot with one of the action groups without completely identifying with it. However, his association was sufficiently close for its rival to try and connect his name with the assassination of one of its student leaders in an act of revenge for a previous killing. Castro made a public statement, accusing his accusers of wishing to destroy him by using the death of a friend and the case against him was dropped.

The sensational deeds of the action groups, however, were only one side of the student scene. The Union of University Students (FEU) of which Castro was a member, during this period followed its historic role of exposing corruption in government by calling a students' strike for the removal of the Minister of Education. It was his Ministry that was referred to in the report in 1951 of an international investigation by the World Bank as 'the principal centre of political patronage and graft' while one ex-Minister of Education described the Ministry as 'an asylum of gunmen'.

In 1948, Fidel Castro was elected president of the Law Association and in this capacity had close contact with the wider world of Latin American student politics, when he helped the students' union organise a conference in Bogota, Columbia, with a view to forming an Anti-Imperialist Latin American Student Association. During the days of the conference, rioting broke out in Bogota in outrage at the killing of the leader of the Columbian left by a hired assassin in the centre of the city and Cuban students, including Fidel Castro, were cited as being involved in the rioting.

The five eventful university years ended with strikes and demonstrations with Fidel Castro in the thick of student support for a bus strike against increased fares. In 1950 he left the university with a degree in civil and diplomatic law and opened a law office in Old Havana where his first clients were students, the Association of Coal Workers, and market stall vendors.

The Moncada attack

After the death of the liberal politician Eduardo Chibás, Fidel Castro stood unsuccessfully as candidate for his Orthodox People's Party but the younger section of that party became increasingly convinced that events had reached a stage in Cuba which ruled out all hope of a parliamentary road to freedom. They argued that the infighting and personal ambition of public figures made it clear that the legal political parties were incapable of overthrowing the dictator. Therefore in the year that followed Batista's coup, young people of Fidel Castro's generation began secretly to prepare for more drastic action by recruiting and training combatants for armed struggle.

Looking back on this time in 1973, Fidel Castro posed the question: 'How were we to carry out an armed insurrection given the fact that the tyranny was all powerful, with its modern means of war and the support of Washington? With the workers' movement shattered and its official leadership at this time in the hand of gangsters sold body and soul to the exploiting class, with the parties of democratic and liberal leanings inarticulate and leaderless, the Marxist party isolated and repressed, McCarthyism at its height, the people with no arms and military experience, with the traditions of armed struggle more than a century away and the myth put around that no revolution could be successful against the established military apparatus: In view of all this, how were we

43

we to do it? How raise the people, how bring them into revolutionary combat to overcome the enervating political crisis and save the country from the exhaustion and terrible backwardness produced by the traitorous coup of March 10th?' He explained: 'We had no economic reserves, no arms, but we started with the thesis that the revolutionary arms were in Cuba, perfectly stored and kept in army posts. And it was from there that we had to seize the arms they had in the forts to start the revolutionary struggle. We planned an attack on the main fort in Santiago de Cuba, and another in Bayamo... The idea was to produce a provincial uprising... We would capture the arms from the enemy, and then use radio stations to win the support of the masses of the whole country.'

The attack on the Moncada Barracks in Santiago was timed to take place on 26th July 1953 in the centenary year of the birth of José Martí, often referred to as its 'intellectual author'. (The date later provided the name of the new 26th July Movement.) One of the largest groups preparing themselves militarily and politically for the attack met in Artemesia at the house of Abel Santamaría and his sister Haydée Santamaría. Abel, who worked as an accountant in a sugar mill, was, with Castro, co-leader of the Moncada project. It is certain that, as part of their political training, Abel Santamaría's group discussed Martí's teachings to which many of their generation were increasingly attracted because his aims corresponded with their own. They shared his belief that liberty was an essential part of man's dignity and they shared his faith that 'no weapon, no force is capable of overcoming a people determined to fight for its rights'. Some also accepted his maxim: 'To die is nothing. He who dies where he should die lives.' (Abel Santamaría was himself killed at Moncada.)

The story has been told many times and in many ways. On July 24th 1953, a chosen number of revolutionaries travelled by bus, train and car to lodgings in an unknown destination. They lodged overnight in Santiago de Cuba and at midnight they proceeded to a small two-acre farm, El

Siboney, on the road to Siboney Beach a few kilometres away from the Sierra Maestra mountains and within easy reach of Santiago de Cuba. The empty farmhouse had been acquired from a sympathiser and here weapons had been previously collected in a well. In the few remaining hours of darkness weapons and uniforms were distributed and plans outlined for the morrow. The main attack would be against the Moncada Barracks of Santiago de Cuba with a simultaneous attack taking place on the army barracks in the town of Bayamo to prevent military reinforcements being sent to Santiago de Cuba. Camouflaged in army uniforms, the plan was to take advantage of the moment when the soldiers were sleeping off the effects of the celebration during the feast of Santa Ana.

A little while before the hour of departure, Fidel Castro spoke briefly to the men and women. Then at 4.45 a.m. on July 26th 1953 around one hundred and thirty-five Cubans dressed in official army uniform with two women as medical aides and a physician, set forth on the road to Santiago de Cuba. Police records show that most of them were sons of working people – small artisans, factory and farm workers, accountants and shop assistants. With them were some teachers and other young professional people and they came from all parts of the island. The plan was to divide into three for the attack. the main contingent with Fidel Castro to undertake the building where the troops were stationed; a small group led by Raúl Castro to occupy the Palace of Justice and another group including the group physician, Abel Santamaría, his sister Haydée Santamaría and her friend Dr. Melba Hernández to take over the hospital. The cars carrying the armed assailants moved forward without difficulty through the holiday crowds still lingering in the streets but at the entrance to the main garrison, things began to go wrong. First the car carrying the best weapons lost its way in the city then an unlucky encounter with a patrol caused some premature firing and the whole barracks was alerted. Accounts vary but it seems very few were killed in the actual fighting. It was during the week that followed that the real bloodshed came when about seventy of the rebels who were taken prisoner, were either shot or died under torture until 'tremendous protest of the people' led by the Archdeacon of Santiago de Cuba called a halt to the slaughter.

A rare glimpse is given of the personal cost and the significance of the Moncada for those who took part in the reminiscences of Haydée Santamaría. In *The Twelve* by Carlos Franqui, she relates her stunned reception of the news that her brother and fiancé had been tortured and shot: 'At Moncada I suffered so much for a while that I became numb to it all. Abel was dead, Boris was dead and I did not even cry. I was feeling nothing. We were unprepared for so much horror . . . From that moment on I thought nothing except of Fidel who could not die, who must stay alive to carry on the Revolution, of Fidel's life which was the life of all of us.'

It was a friendly sergeant, Pedro Sarria, who found Castro in the mountains to which he had escaped with seventeen others, recognised him and, acting on his belief that 'ideas cannot be murdered', probably saved his life by having him transferred to a civil rather than a military prison. In the trial that followed sentences of fifteen years were passed on Fidel Castro and thirteen years on his younger brother, Raúl, with shorter sentences for the other defendants. (Public opinion, in fact, secured an amnesty for the prisoners after only two years.)

'History will absolve me'

During the secret trial an attempt was made to prevent Castro appearing in court, by means of the false witness of prison doctors. However, one of the women accused, Dr Melba Hernández, managed to smuggle out of prison a letter from him which contained a statement to the court to the effect that he was in perfect health. In the end he not only appeared at the trial but conducted his own defence in a famous speech which was later printed on a secret press by women members of the 26th July Movement and distributed throughout the island under the title *History will absolve me.*

The Moncada attack has been described as the little wheel that set the big wheels turning. It is, however, clear from the very first manifesto of the Moncada revolutionaries that they believed a successful revolution could only be made by the mass of the people who must provide its driving force. 'Above all,' the manifesto declared, 'This must be a revolution of the people, with the blood of the people and the sweat of the people.'

At his trial Fidel Castro precisely defined this use of the word 'people': 700,000 Cubans without work, 500,000 farm labourers 'who work only for four months of the year', 400,000 industrial workers and stevedores 'whose homes are hovels', 100,000 small farmers 'who live and die working on land they do not own', 30,000 teachers and professors 'badly paid and treated', 10,000 small business men 'ruined by crisis', 10,000 young professionals 'at a dead end with all doors closed . . . These are the people, the ones who know misfortune and, therefore, are capable of fighting with limitless courage. To the people whose roads through life have been paved with bricks of betrayals and false promises, we are not going to say: we will eventually give you what you need, but rather – here you have it, fight for it with all your might so that liberty and happiness may be yours.'

Already in Castro's defence speech it was clear that at least part of the leadership had come to the conclusion that these goals presupposed profound changes in Cuban society that could only be achieved by challenging the main power bases of the establishment including the law and the army.

GUERRILLA WAR

THE AMNESTY of May 15th 1955 brought to the survivors of the Moncada personal liberty but not the restoration of civil rights. Banned from television and, with the closing down of opposition newspapers, left without a platform for their views, Fidel Castro and a small group of companions left secretly for Mexico, there to prepare the next stage of the campaign – the invasion of Cuba and if necessary a prolonged guerrilla war. On July 7th 1955, Castro sent a letter to prominent political leaders explaining: 'I am leaving Cuba because all doors of peaceful struggle are closed to me. Six weeks after being released from prison I am more convinced than ever of the dictator's decision to remain in power one way or another for twenty years.'

In Mexico, the rebels set about seeking urgently needed funds from exiles both in Latin America and the United States, at the same time forming Patriotic Clubs of the 26th July Movement abroad similar to those formed by José Martí when preparing for struggle a century before. With the money collected in Cuba and abroad, weapons were bought and billets found for some eighty volunteers who had made their way to Mexico. A ranch was acquired in a remote area at the foot of Popacatapetl and here under the supervision of Colonel Alberto Bayo, formerly of the school of military aviation in Cuba, the men were put through an intensive course of training. Among those receiving military training was a young Argentinian doctor recently returned from Latin America – Ernesto Che Guevara. This is how he described to an Argentinian reporter his first meeting with Fidel Castro at this time:

'In Aztec land I saw again some members of the 26th July Movement whom I had known in Guatemala and struck up friendship with Raúl Castro, Fidel Castro's younger brother. He introduced me to the chief of the Movement when they were planning the invasion of Cuba ... I spoke to Fidel a whole night. At dawn I was already the doctor of the future expedition. In reality after the experience I had been through, my long walks throughout Latin America ... not much was needed to convince me to join a revolution against a tyrant but Fidel impressed me as an extraordinary man. He faced and resolved the impossible. He had an unshakeable faith that once he left he would arrive in Cuba, that once he arrived he would fight, that once fighting began he would win. I shared his optimism ... it was essential to stop crying and fight.'

The Granma *expedition*

Finally, after many mishaps including seizure of equipment and terms in Mexican jails, on November 25th 1956 at two o'clock in the morning, in complete darkness, a crew of eighty-three men packed into an old yacht and left Mexico for Cuba. The *Granma* was launched and so was the invasion, for better or for worse.

'Our revolution began under incredible circumstances,' said Fidel Castro in retrospect. In heavy seas amid an 'infernal mess of sick men and materials of all sorts' the yacht lost its bearings and was further delayed by a man going overboard. On November 30th, the day planned for the landing, back in Cuba the civilian wing of the movement had timed various acts of sabotage in Santiago de Cuba to draw attention away from the landing. This part of the plan was carried out on time at considerable cost to those who took part, but the expeditionary force in the *Granma* was still far out at sea. When at length the yacht landed, it stuck in the mud near the beach of Coloradas some distance away from the intended landing place and each man had to make his way through mangrove-covered marshes with whatever he could carry.

Che Guevara in his journal writes. 'Seven days at sea were followed by three terrible days on land. Exactly ten days after leaving Mexico, at dawn of December 5th ... we reached a place known – what a paradox – as Happiness of Pio in the district of Niguero.' Here the exhausted men were resting in a thicket on the edge of a sugar field when a hurricane of bullets fell. Batista's army had been alerted. Fidel Castro gave orders for the men to scatter in small groups but planes hunted them down and later when they reassembled, with Fidel and Raúl Castro and Che Guevara there remained only a handful of the whole invading army of the 26th July Movement.

Staving off hunger by the help of raw turtles, crabs and the juice of sugar cane, the survivors reached Turquino, the highest peak in the Sierra Maestra on December 25th. Asked if he realised it was Christmas, Fidel Castro is said to have answered. 'I do. The days of the tyranny are numbered.' Raúl Castro once said that the most important trait in his brother's character was that he never admitted defeat – for himself or for the revolution. But it was more than unbounded optimism that convinced Fidel Castro on that first Christmas in the Sierra Maestra that a handful of men on a mountain almost without arms and ammunition could succeed against a fully-mechanised army.

It was the knowledge that potential allies existed in almost every section of Cuban people that gave his hopes firm basis. He knew, for instance, before leaving Mexico of the national strike of half a million sugar workers at the end of 1955 when for six days, despite the combined force of police, rural guards and the military, sixty towns near sugar refineries declared themselves 'dead cities' in support of their demands and raised the slogan 'Down with this criminal government'. The two years between those first months wandering in the forests and hills of the Sierra Maestra and the final rout of Batista on New Year's Day 1959 were to provide further proof to the guerrillas that the roots of Cuba's century-old struggle for freedom still ran deep among her people.

'I believe that one of the errors of those first days was the lack of any major exchange of views between the different organisations. Each of us was acting more or less on our own account. It was the revolutionary struggle itself which brought us more and more into contact, more and more into common discussion and steadily promoted our unification.' The main revolutionary organisations referred to here by Fidel Castro in an interview with an Italian newspaper in 1961 were the 26th July Movement of which the Rebel Army was the military wing, the Popular Socialist Party (PSP) as the old Cuban Communist Party was called, and the Students' Revolutionary Directorate based mainly on the universities. At times the three organisations differed profoundly on tactics but Cubans today insist that all three made a weighty contribution towards the final triumph of the revolution. A brief review of each reveals the initial problems which had to be patiently overcome before they merged after victory into what was known as the Integrated Organisations of the Revolution (ORI) which in 1965 formed the basis of the new Communist Party of Cuba.

The 26th July Movement, which took its name from the date of the attack on Fort Moncada, described itself like this in its first manifesto of 1955. 'The 26th July Movement is formed without hatred to anyone. It is not a political party but a revolutionary movement. Its ranks are open to all Cubans who sincerely desire to see political democracy and social justice introduced in Cuba. Its leadership is collective and secret, formed by new men of strong will who are not accomplices of the past. Its structure is functional. Young and old, men and women, students and professionals can join its fighting units, its youth cadres, its secret workers' cells, its women's organisations, its economic section and its underground distribution apparatus throughout the country, for not all can take up arms.' Its programme at the time of Moncada included honesty in public life, agrarian reform, a public health service of preventative medicine, nationalisation of U.S.-owned electricity and telephones, restoration of the Constitution of 1940 and elections. 'It was not a Socialist programme,' Fidel Castro said later (1974), 'but it was the best programme we could realistically put forward at that time.' Its activists were mainly young people in their teens and early twenties but members were of all ages and social classes and included some who, though prepared to unite to rid Cuba of Batista, were opposed to communism.

The Popular Socialist Party even when outlawed and comparatively isolated kept its influence among sections of the rank and file trade unionists. In 1951, during a period when the party was legal, the committee which prepared the report on Cuba for the international World Bank had this to say of its members: 'It was the superior industriousness, devotion, training and tactical skill of the Communists which enabled them to establish decisive influence in the Cuban labour movement.'

Soon after Batista's coup, the PSP issued a manifesto calling for a united front and mass struggle to achieve a democratic solution to the crisis. It differed from Fidel Castro and the 26th July Movement on the tactic of armed struggle – its timing and use. In the round up of suspects following the attack on the Moncada and Bayamo barracks, its Santiago headquarters was ransacked, the party outlawed and forced to work underground. In point of fact its members were not involved in either of the attacks. On the contrary the leadership publicly criticised the action as 'an adventurist attempt guided by mistaken bourgeois conceptions'. Some of its leaders were also critical of the resort to arms at the time of the *Granma* landing, believing that the armed movement was premature while its acts of associated terror gave excuse to police repression in which thousands of homes were raided and citizens imprisoned.

By the beginning of 1958, most of these differences had been sorted out. From then on until the end of the war, the party's representative Carlos Raphael Rodríguez remained in the Sierra Maestra headquarters of the Rebel Army and Communist detachments linked up with Che Guevara in Las Villas. It was Che who rebuked an anti-communist interviewer of the New York *Tribune* by remarking: 'I will tell you this, though I am no communist, I did not see your newspaper or you when the Communists were fighting and dying at our side in the Sierra.'

Looking back self-critically on this period after victory, the secretary of the Popular Socialist Party publicly stated that his party had been mistaken in being unprepared for armed struggle and it was 'Fidel Castro's historical merit that he prepared, trained and assembled the fighting elements needed to carry on armed struggle.'

Cuban students, true to their traditions, were among the first to raise their voice against the dictatorship. At the time of Fidel Castro's departure to Mexico, several leaders of the University Students Union (FEU) met secretly to analyse events. Led by their president, a Catholic student José A. Echevarría, the group decided to prepare the ground for armed struggle and a wave of student marches and demonstrations, violent and non-violent, swept the island, merging in 1955 with the extensive strike of the sugar workers. About this time, the revolutionists of the FEU revived the *Revolutionary Directorate* of the 'thirties and José Echevarría went to Mexico for discussions with Fidel Castro who was then preparing the *Granma* expedition. According to accounts, they were in complete agreement that armed struggle had become essential but they differed somewhat on the form it should take. The Student Directorate favoured 'striking at the top' with the assassination of major political figures culminating in the assassination of Batista. Castro argued that this approach would only do away with men and not destroy the system because it would leave existing institutions untouched. It was agreed to support each other and keep in touch while the organisations worked independently. (Later during the revolutionary war the Directorate had its own guerrilla detachment mainly based in the Escambray mountains.)

In January of the eventful year 1957, Batista suspended civil rights. On March 13th of the same year, on the initiative of the Student Directorate, some fifty men – students in their early twenties together with veterans of the Spanish Civil War and members of past action groups – attacked the Presidential Palace in Havana with the hope of finding a quick end to the war. The plan was to assassinate Batista and take possession of the civic building. The guards were taken by surprise, and in the fighting and general confusion, some assailants managed to reach Batista's office on the second floor only to find it empty. By then tanks and troops had surrounded the building and the attackers were mown down as they tried to escape. José Echevarría was himself killed after having made a simultaneous attack on a radio station. Today in Cuba the attack on the Presidential Palace is honoured in the revolutionary calendar along with other events that are seen as a heroic contribution to the final triumph of the revolution.

Broad unity of the opposition finally became the main strength of the anti-Batista struggle. Besides the three revolutionary organisations, the opposition to the dictatorship included a group linked with Carlos Prío, an emigré leader of an old type conservative political party, the Auténticos, with support in some sections of Cuba's business community.

The city resistance

The underground struggles in the cities and plains, according to the 26th July Movement, took a total toll of twenty thousand lives. Even if this is a very inflated figure all accounts put the cost very high. An eye witness Teresa Caruso wrote: 'Every sunrise revealed dozens of corpses ... The most barbaric methods of torture, not excluding castration, were daily incidents in the police stations where the groans of a whole generation of youths were heard as they were tortured for information or for having aided the revolutionary movement.'

Perhaps the greatest individual loss to the movement in 1957 was the death of Frank País of Santiago who had formed a strong underground organisation in Oriente with its own clandestine newspaper and policy based on generalised armed struggle in the mountains and cities culminating in a well-organised general strike that would drive Batista from power. Later the group agreed to merge with the 26th July Movement and Frank País became national coordinator of civic resistance. Betrayed by an informer, Frank País was assassinated on July 30th 1957. On the day of his funeral, Santiago became a city of mourning as a workers' strike closed down shops and industry not only in Oriente but in Camagüey and parts of Las Villas. A contemporary report in the newspaper *El Mundo* describes how the following day, when the U.S. ambassador visited Santiago de Cuba to take stock of the situation, two hundred women dressed in black presented a petition against the regime's 'reign of terror' and as they began to shout 'Freedom' the police charged the demonstrators who were so manhandled that the ambassador himself deplored 'the excessive use of force' by the police.

Total War

Meanwhile a new stage had been reached in the Sierra. Major Raúl Castro with a column of sixty-eight men successfully opened a second front in the mountains of the north-east of Oriente, known as the Frank País Front, and here before the end of the war the rebels, supported by a strong movement among the peasants in the area, were in control of about six thousand acres and joined by many recruits.

Cubans listening to Radio Rebelde on March 12th 1958

heard Fidel Castro broadcast from 'the free territory of Cuba' a manifesto from the 26th July Movement to the people. It called for intensified revolutionary action and preparation for a general strike. It appealed to Batista's army to rebel and at the same time gave notice of the invasion to the north and east of Cuba by rebel forces. 'As from this instant, the country should consider itself in total war against the tyranny.'

The 1958 general strike, while solid in towns like Santiago and Camagüey, was weak and disunited in Havana. Che Guevara later passed the opinion that this was partly due to inadequate planning and partly because the workers most affected did not have enough say in the planning and timing over which there seems to have been some confusion. As a result 'a great and select number of people were assassinated mercilessly'.

Following the strike, while Fidel Castro, broadcasting from the Sierra Maestra, reasoned and urged people to throw off despair, Batista seized the opportunity to announce an all out attack which he declared would wipe out the Rebel Army.

In torrential rain, ten thousand soldiers in fourteen battallions and seven companies equipped with modern weapons converged on all sides towards the mountain range of the Sierra Maestra where the Rebel Army had its headquarters. Against them the rebel's eight columns positioned themselves on a fifteen mile front so as to guard all approaches to the mountains. They numbered only a few hundred but the guerrillas were on home ground, sure of their cause and by now had strong links with the country people.

For the first thirty days Batista's troops gained ground under cover of a heavy air bombardment. Gradually, however, as the government troops penetrated further into the mountains they became disorientated. Frequently ambushed, they were constantly cut off from supply routes of food and ammunition besides being drenched and delayed by the rains of the hurricane season. Meanwhile loud hailers promised them safe conduct if they went over to the side of their people.

On July 29th 1958 government forces in Santo Domingo suffered particularly large casualties, losing several hundred prisoners to the rebels. Soon after this setback, the government offensive ended and the command was given to all government troops to withdraw. This order was followed by a retreat that soon turned into a disorderly rout in which precious arms, food and medicine supplies were left behind. The defeat was broadcast throughout Cuba on the rebel radio over which Fidel Castro now spoke almost daily to the Cuban people. Very soon after the retreat the Rebel Army launched their counter offensive and the decision was taken to pursue the route of Antonio Maceo, carrying the invasion across the country from east to west in such a way as to cut the island in two and disrupt the enemy's communication lines.

Two columns of crack troops headed by Che Guevara and Camilo Cienfuegos carried out this feat in one-and-a-half months. Major Camilo Cienfuegos, Cuba's popular hero of the revolutionary war, whose plane was lost at sea in the first year of victory, wrote in his diary:

'For fifteen days we went through water and mud up to our knees spending nights avoiding ambushes from troops . . . during thirty-one days travel across Camagüey Province, we ate only eleven times. We had to kill and eat a mare (raw and unsalted) from our meagre cavalry . . . Almost all our animals remained behind in the mud and marshes of our coast.'

But volunteers all along the way joined the column and on Christmas Eve 1958 a rebel radio station broadcast the news that Guevara's forces had taken the city of Sancti Spiritus in Las Villas Province. On Christmas Day the troops of Raúl and Fidel Castro marched on Santiago de Cuba in Oriente and on New Year's Day, Batista saw the writing on the wall and fled.

After the discovery of a plot between army officers in Havana and the commander of Batista's military forces in

Oriente who had pursued negotiations as a delaying tactic enabling Batista to escape, the rebel command announced by radio that war would continue until there was unconditional surrender and called on the Cuban people to prepare for a national strike and general insurrection as soon as they received word from Radio Rebelde.

This time a totally successful strike shut down virtually all industry and commerce and, before dawn on January 2nd 1958, Major Castro's column marched on Santiago de Cuba to accept unconditional surrender of Batista's forces at Fort Moncada. Photo-reports of the time show the crowds wild with joy as the bearded victorious army rode in triumph from one end of the island to the other, 'shouting their admiration and affection for their thirty-two-year-old hero at its head and acclaiming him by popular consent leader of the nation.'

FROM NATIONAL LIBERATION TO SOCIALISM

IT WAS a feature of the Cuban Revolution that its foremost leaders who had fought under the banner of the 26th July Movement were non-communists who developed into Marxists in the course of the revolution as the revolution itself deepened from one of national liberation to a socialist revolution.

Unlike the Russian and Chinese, the Cuban revolutionaries did not inherit a country devastated by long years of war. They did, however, inherit between six and seven hundred thousand unemployed out of a work force of two and a half million, and an economy that had more or less stood still for the last thirty years while the population had doubled, so that although the average wage was high by the low Latin American standards, there were sectors of great poverty. They also inherited problems of underdevelopment in a tropical climate where summer heat was unconducive to long hours of heavy labour, in an island whose only sources of energy were limited stocks of timber. Cuba had no coal or steel of her own, nor great rivers as sources of hydro-electric energy – a fact that made her at that time very dependent on her main trading partner, North America. So all in all, it was soon realised that beyond the days of national rejoicing lay problems as complicated as any met with in the Sierra.

The immediate problem of preventing sabotage by the supporters of the old regime partially solved itself by many of their number fleeing the country. Warning had been given to those who served in Batista's state bureaucracy as early as March of 1958. The National Directorate meeting at the Sierra Maestra headquarters of the Rebel Army broadcast its unanimous agreement that 'The continuance of any person in office of trust in the executive branch from the presidency of the government councils to paragovernmental agencies subsequent to April 5th will be considered treason to the fatherland ... Also due to the state of war between the people of Cuba and the Batista Tyranny, any officer, or enlisted man in the army who continues to render service against the oppressed people after April 5th will lose his right to continue service in the armed forces ... Likewise any judicial functionary, magistrate or attorney who wishes to preserve his right to continue in office must immediately resign because lack of guarantees and respect for legal procedure has converted the judiciary into a useless body.'

Remembering the scenes of mob vengeance after the fall of another dictator, the Rebel Army leaders issued a public order that no citizen however wronged must take justice into their own hands but all could rest assured that justice would be done. Revolutionary tribunals were set up to which public and press had access to try 'war criminals' i.e. those who were known to have been killers and torturers on behalf of Batista's regime. The families of those who had suffered were given an opportunity to give evidence and in all some six hundred death sentences were passed – a verdict upheld as just by most Cubans but creating an outcry abroad particularly in the United States.

Congress with its history of corrupt government was abolished. Some new provisional governmental bodies were created and, after the first few months revolutionaries, mainly Rebel Army men were appointed to positions of power. Ministers of the First Revolutionary Council were mostly men under thirty-five years of age with service in the revolutionary armed forces. At first Fidel Castro limited his government role to head of the new Revolutionary Armed Forces but on February 13th 1959 he accepted the post of Prime Minister of Cuba. Five months later he resigned on account of policy differences with the first president of the revolutionary government, a liberal lawyer Manuela Urrutia. He withdrew his resignation, however, when the Council of Ministers appointed Dr Osvaldo Dorticós as president. (Dr

Dorticós and Dr Castro have worked together as President and Prime Minister of Cuba to this day.) A feature of their government was dialogue between leaders and people in frequent mass meetings, thousands strong, where government policy was outlined in detail and accepted by popular acclaim.

Because of Cuba's history of broken promises, the Cuban revolutionaries decided it was essential to provide immediate visible signs of change by ironing out some of the contrasts in Cuban society: contrasts between very rich and very poor, between black and white, between the numbers out of work and the large areas of land lying idle. These early reforms had almost universal approval. An imaginative construction programme of schools, clinics, houses, roads and recreation centres was directed to the underdeveloped countryside with the aim of bringing amenities before known mainly in the disproportionately developed capital. During the early months of 1959 Year of Liberation the Government halved all rents in the island, and afterwards farm rents were abolished. Many acres of unused land were cleaned and ploughed and as a result of this expanding building, agricultural and industrial programme unemployment virtually disappeared so that in 1962 in the countryside there began to be a shortage of labour. The total wage bill also considerably increased. This together with free medical services and free canteen meals in schools and cheap ones in work places meant that many rural families had more to spend on consumer goods than ever before in their lives. In the first three years this had a stimulating effect on the economy. Later, when production failed to keep pace and the U.S. blockade cut off traditional trade routes, shortages, transport problems and food rationing began to appear. As Cuban leaders have frankly stated, initial mistakes in industrial policy aggravated the situation. One of these was too speedy and too general diversification of agriculture at the expense of Cuba's chief currency raising crop – sugar. This led later to a thorough review of farming policy in which the emphasis was again restored to Cuba's traditional export crops but variety was retained by regional specialisation in citrus fruit, pineapples, rice etc.

Increasingly, as they tackled the tasks facing them, the Cuban revolutionary leaders became convinced that fundamental changes in the pattern of society were needed to make planned development possible and in this they still had the enthusiastic support of the majority of Cuban people. An American sociologist, Maurice Zeitling, deduced from a questionnaire carried out among a sample number of workers in different parts of the island in 1962 that 142 out of 202 supported the Revolutionary Government, 24 were undecided and 36 were hostile. But as reforms cut deeper into the structure of society and challenged the economic roots of foreign control, opinion abroad became alarmed especially in America. This alarm was shared by a minority of Cuban people, especially after the agrarian reform laws which fixed the maximum size of privately-owned farms and nationalised land in excess of this amount, distributing a proportion to landless peasants. Some began to plot against the Revolutionary Government, others for a mixture of reasons, not all political, decided to part company with the new Cuba and among these were much needed doctors, university professors, and other skilled people. Government policy was to arrange air travel to Miami for those wishing to emigrate so that all who stayed in Cuba did so of their own free will but before leaving applicants were required to serve a period in agriculture or other productive work. Over the years, this exodus drained away a great many Cubans and much skill and experience from Cuba. Some opponents of the revolution who stayed on in Cuba organised armed resistance in guerrilla bands centred mainly in the region of the Escambray mountains. Among those tried for counter-revolutionary plotting as early as 1959 and given heavy prison sentences was Hubert Matos. He was a popular major in the Sierra Maestra who after Victory was appointed provincial military governor – a post he resigned, calling on others to follow his example, in protest at what he saw as Cuba's headlong rush to communism.

1960 and 1961 were years of particularly rapid change when many privately owned properties passed into public hands. During this period Cuba had to face a total blockade, an invasion and a complete changeover of trading partners from the United States close at hand to Russia and the socialist countries thousands of miles away. The following is a calendar of events – the barest outline of a complex and far reaching process by which the Cuban people came to own the main resources of their country and so were able, as it seemed to them, for the first time in history to begin to plan their use for the majority of its inhabitants.

May 17th 1959. The first agrarian reform law confiscates the estates of Batista's supporters and others who fled the country and fixes the maximum size of privately-owned farms at one thousand acres. (Later a second reform law reduced the maximum size of private farms to one hundred and sixty-four acres.)

May 17th 1959. Che Guevara signs economic and cultural agreements with Egypt, India, Pakistan, Indonesia and Japan.

February 4th 1960. A commercial treaty is signed in Havana between Cuba and Russia who offers oil at a preferential price. Standard Oil Texaco and Shell who manage Cuban oil refuse to refine 'red petroleum'.

March 4th 1960. An explosion takes place on a French ship *Le Courbre* carrying arms for Cuba from Belgium and causes nearly a hundred deaths. Cuba lays the blame on the Central Intelligence Agency of America (CIA).

May 8th 1960. Diplomatic relations between Cuba and Soviet Union are resumed.

July 5th 1960. The United States refuses to buy the residue of Cuba's 1960 sugar quota i.e. 700,000 tons.

July 9th 1960. The Soviet Government agree to buy sugar that the Americans will not take.

July 23rd 1960. First commercial treaty between China and Cuba is signed.

August 6th 1960. A law is passed by which the government nationalises all U.S.-owned properties in agriculture including thirty-six sugar mills and refineries, as well as the telephone company with a proposed compensation of 4.5% over twenty years indemnification.

August 15th 1960. At a meeting of the Organisation of American States in Latin America, the United States sponsors a resolution condemning Cuba's rapprochement with the socialist countries.

September 3rd 1960. Fidel Castro replies by calling a national assembly of all Cuba when about a million people in Revolution Square endorsed an eight point document known as the First Declaration of Havana. It condemned the 'open intervention of North American imperialism for more than a century in the affairs of Latin America' and stressed the right to self-determination of Latin American peoples, denying that help received from the Soviet and Chinese help was in any way aimed at endangering the unity of the hemisphere. Finally it reaffirmed Cuba's policy of friendship with all people, including the people of the United States and emphasised Cuba's intention 'to trade with all the world and not just part of it'.

October 15th 1960. The Revolutionary Government nationalises three hundred and eighty-two large private enterprises and banks, including Cuban-owned sugar mills and cane lands in joint ownership.

October 19th 1960. The United States breaks off relations with Cuba. In preparation for the landing of an emigré expeditionary force claiming the backing of the United States, raiders make lightning raids on Havana and Santiago airports with seven dead and fifty-three civilians wounded. Fidel Castro calls for the formation of committees for the defence of the revolution and arms the people's militia.

April 16th 1961. Speaking at the funeral of the victims,

Castro for the first time makes public reference to Cuba having entered the Socialist phase of her revolution.

April 17th 1961: At 1 a.m. invasion forces some fifteen hundred strong, and including about two hundred of Batista's former militia and police force, land at the beach head at Playa Girón in the Bay of Pigs on the south coast of Cuba, calling upon the Cubans to revolt. Small local militia units resist until the Cuban armed forces arrive consisting of large land forces and a very small air force. Major Fidel Castro and the army command direct operations from a near-by sugar mill. By the evening of April 19th Playa Girón has fallen, with over a thousand prisoners taken and the news is broadcast: 'The Revolution is victorious. It destroyed in less than seventy-two hours the invading army organised by the imperialist Government of the United States during many months.'

April 25th 1961: The United States declares a total embargo on all trade with Cuba.

December 2nd 1961: Fidel Castro proclaims: 'I am a Marxist Leninist and I shall remain one all the rest of my life.' At the same time he called for the formation of a unified party of the socialist revolution from the three main organisations that led the anti-Batista struggle. (The United Party of the Socialist Revolution in 1963 replaced the Integrated Revolutionary Organisations (ORI) and later in 1965 was itself merged into the new Communist Party of Cuba).

Cuba was on the road to becoming the first socialist state in Latin America and the Western hemisphere. The rest of this book seeks to examine some of the effects of this historic change particularly on the lives of children and young people met by the author during a three-month visit to Cuba in the autumn of 1971 and a return visit in March-April of 1975.

PART II
Havana Diary

FIRST IMPRESSIONS

LOOKING BACK on a three months' visit to Cuba thirteen years
after the victory of the 1959 revolution, there are certain
things for which I am particularly grateful. In Havana's
Hotel Riviera, large windows open on to the Caribbean so
that the sea was a constant link between all that happened
in Havana, a background to talks and filling in the hours
when nothing was planned, unbelievably beautiful at full
moon, at sunset, at dawn. I was fortunate too to be visiting
as a children's writer because the Cuban's warm affection for
children guaranteed a response to my special interest, and
interviews were informal, flexible and rewarding. Lastly and
chiefly, I count myself privileged in the quality of the friends
who acted as hosts and interpreters of the new Cuba.

I met Monica on the first morning after an early breakfast
served in the fresh air in the shade of palms and I can see her
now as she sat chatting with her back to the sea. She was a
fair-haired twenty-six-year-old Cuban of German extraction
with two children, one at a nursery and the other attending
a weekly boarding school while she herself did a very full-
time job for the Cuban Women's Federation. Over the weeks
that I was in Monica's care I was to learn much about her
generation of young people by studying her. It was clear that
she identified so entirely with Cuba's revolution and its
achievements that she was able to look cooly at its short-
comings and was indeed insisting that I do the same in order
to see the situation as a whole. The effect was to give reality
to our talks and while we spoke most about the subject of my
visit – Cuban children – no subject was taboo. Monica's
lively mind paid interested attention to my comments but I
could feel she made allowance for the fact that they came
from someone who lived in the consumer-orientated society

of the old capitalist world whose values Cuba had discarded.

Despite the shortage of cars and drivers, 'English punc-tuality' as the Cubans call it was a feature of an imaginative programme organised by Monica and her young colleague Celia of the Cultural Council. One of our first visits was to the Ana Betancourt schools for peasant girls and our early morning conversation related to my query. why a school in Havana for the daughters of peasants?

The reason lies in the backwardness and underdevelop-ment of the Cuban countryside when the revolution took over and its special repercussion on women. The contrast between the amenities of the cities where most upper-class people lived and the neglected rural areas can be seen in Ministry figures for school attendance in 1942-43. While over sixty-eight per cent of children ages five to thirteen attended primary school in Havana, only twenty per cent went to school in Oriente, the most heavily populated province with a third of the nation's children. UNESCO's *World Survey of Education*, quoting a report prepared by the Cuban Ministry of Education in 1956, states that 'the fact of a child's home being more than two kilometres from school may be regarded as adequate reason for non-attendance. Attendance is much lower in rural areas than in towns, the chief reason for non-attendance being lack of means.' The same report mentions re-organisation of rural education in 1952 and the building of forty rural central schools with accommodation for thirty boarders, but the census for the following year showed that still only a little over a quarter of Oriente's children went to school.

A Cuban agricultural inspector Alejandro Fernandez de Cueto made a special study of conditions in the remote coffee producing area of Cienfuegos-Trinidad in 1945. His report is given in full in Lowry Nelson's *Rural Cuba**. The inspector found that in the whole large region there was no church.

Rural Cuba by Lowry Nelson, University of Minnesota Press 1950. Lowry Nelson was appointed rural sociologist in the United States Department of State in September 1945.

Children were baptised in groups at the price of three dollars a child. Well-to-do farmers had church weddings but common-law marriage was most frequent. There was no doctor, no lawyer, no library, no newspaper, no banks and no telegraph, and for the most part no form of latrine sanitary or insanitary. In cases of illness the sick were treated by home remedies and in serious cases they were carried to the city 'this being very costly since they had to stop at hotels'. Principal means of communication was by mule train, poor provision of roads making farms inaccessible in the rainy season.

In these deprived rural areas, the peasant woman suffered most from the poverty and isolation from which there was virtually no escape. The Constitution of 1940, enlightened in many respects, contained a clause on sex equality but as long as unemployment remained, few dignified jobs were open to women. While the situation within the Cuban family varied according to class and race, society continued to take it for granted that the woman should spend her life in the narrow confines of her home, reproducing and rearing its future citizens. At the same time, the influence of the old patriarchal family code inherited centuries ago from feudal Spain still demanded her subordinate and submissive role as wife and mother. (This influence lingered on a long time and until the new law of 1918, almost the only reason for divorce was, to quote Article 105 'Adultery of the wife in any case, and of the husband when it results in public scandal or neglect of his wife . . .'.)

The revolutionary government felt that emergency action was essential to help those who were the worst sufferers from colonialism's legacy of ignorance and superstition and still young enough to adapt to a new life. In the first years, three crash educational programmes were organised by Cuban women for women. In the cities, some twenty thousand former domestic servants registered in classes to train for new careers, while those of Havana's prostitutes that chose to remain in Cuba were offered social and educational help to start a new life. For peasant women in the remote rural areas new horizons opened with the creation of a school for peasant girls in Havana.

A school for peasant girls

Fifth Avenue as its name suggests was once the gracious centre of Havana's fashionable suburbia but driving along its tree-lined length in the early 'seventies one met everywhere groups of school girls, for this area then formed part of the Ana Betancourt school community. (Ana Betancourt was a woman's rights campaigner and freedom fighter of the last century.) Here a school complex of more than three hundred residencies provided boarding school accommodation for girls from the country. In the cool front room of one of these houses the school managers told the full story.

The experiment began in 1961 when the Ana Betancourt school was started for peasant families living in areas where schooling was practically non-existent. In the first year under the direction of the Federation of Cuban Women, about a thousand girls aged sixteen to twenty came from the Sierra Maestra region to attend classes first held in the Habana Libre Hotel. One of the teachers Professor Berta Hernandez Moralez later recalled the experience: 'I shall never forget the day I arrived at Habana Libre Hotel to see my peasant sisters, born in the very heart of the Sierra Maestra, who because of the remoteness of their homes used to come to us with fear in their faces. The instinct of flight was so strong in them that when they saw me they ran barefoot through the carpeted corridors, hiding in the rooms in groups as if playing a subtle game of hide and seek.'

The emphasis was at first on dressmaking, which was seen as the thin edge of the wedge in order to win the parents' essential support for the scheme. This was not easy because the whole weight of tradition was against the girls moving outside the confines of the home circle and rumours were spread that the revolution was luring them away. It was therefore felt that confidence would be more easily won if the parents knew that the first skills taught would be of direct benefit in the home. But some reading, writing and arithmetic was taught even in the first year. At the end of the course, all girls left with a sewing machine and took back with them new outlooks and habits which could be an example and help to the rest of the village community. The girls had become accustomed to consulting a doctor, having regular dental treatment and learning about first aid and general hygiene. Meanwhile parents had come to visit their daughters, seen they were safe with undreamed of opportunities and they too began to share their children's confidence in the new Cuba.

In 1962 the intake was fourteen hundred girls of fourteen and upwards most of whom were very much below their age in school learning. Emphasis was still on dressmaking but the next year a full primary school curriculum was started for these elder girls and by 1964, with an intake of ten thousand, dressmaking was only one subject within a primary school curriculum. Two years later children of seven were following a normal primary school education and for the first time there was also a group of secondary school pupils.

'With the development of the Revolution came changes in the original plan of the Ana Betancourt Schools,' explained the chairman of the managers. 'The great need in the new society was for teachers – particularly in those isolated mountain areas from which the children came, where previously to find a teacher had been like hunting for a needle in a haystack. This need the Ana Betancourt community decided to fill. A new experiment transformed it into a pupil-teacher training centre. Immediately a pupil reached sixth grade or secondary level she undertook to pass her knowledge on to those who knew less. So it now became the usual thing to see girls taking classes with the help of the teacher at all levels of the school. Apart from valuable experience in teaching, it has other good effects. The students have to revise constantly and truly understand their subject in order to pass it on to others.'

After this background briefing we spent the rest of the day with the children and teachers. Some of the villas have been converted into 'houses of culture'. Here the girls, according to aptitude and interest, can specialise in the art and sport of their choice. water ballet and swimming, dancing and music, theatre and painting. One group of older girls specialised in the crafts and sciences related to textiles, spending part of their time in a textile factory as a preparation to further qualifying as textile specialists.

Our first visit was to a long low villa which in the 'thirties General Gerardo Machado was said to have bought from funds misappropriated from charities. Children's flower paintings decorated the school notice boards on either side of a verandah and class-rooms opened off a central patio filled with growing plants. In one of these a thirteen-year-old was taking a lesson under teacher supervision on the use of wood, bone and skin in the ancient crafts of Cuba. In another larger room opening on to a leafy garden, eight and nine-year-olds were painting at easels with large brushes and jars of paint. The week of my arrival, Cuban children all over Cuba were remembering the anniversaries of Che Guevara and Camilo Cienfuegos whose photographs one saw everywhere, and it was the story of the two national heroes that the children were painting. (There was one exception, a vivid green and brown painting of climbing monkeys.)

I left with two pictures as a present from these second grade children. One was a painting of Che Guevara with his guerrillas and their guns on the topmost peaks of the Andes of Bolivia where he met his death in 1968 (Plate XX). The other was a painting of a row of children looking over the sea wall at the waves. On these floated pink, red, blue, purple flowers thrown into the water as children do every year for Camilo Cienfuegos whose plane was said to have been lost at sea in the first year of victory (Plate IV).

An evening visit

The early evening was spent with the collective of a house

74

converted into a hostel for twenty-nine children of ages ranging from seven to fourteen. There were on average about eight beds to every bedroom with a pupil teacher in each dormitory and a member of the teaching staff sleeping in the house overnight. There was a quiet room with six small rocking chairs in which the children took turns to sit, and a playroom gay with paper mobiles and some toys made by a group of factory workers for the national distribution of toys which takes place every year on Children's Day. Scarcity of materials meant toys were scarce and often had to be shared one to a group, but I noticed a bedtime doll tucked under the counterpane of each of the younger children's beds.

The housemother was a vivacious young teacher from Havana. 'These people from Oriente,' she said, 'they may not chatter as much as we do in Havana but they think and feel deeply. You can see it in their faces.' Surrounded by shining eyes and eloquent faces I could see what she meant. I asked did they miss their homes in the country and mountains? No, they laughed. Quite the opposite. When they were home too long they missed the school. The housemother explained: 'At times, particularly at first, some parents don't want to bring their children back and we have to respect this. But generally, though the children are happy to go home for the month's holiday, they soon want to come back even before the month is up. Living like this in a group, a very strong community spirit is developed and it is this I think they miss most. This lot has been together for a year now and already it is turning into a very nice collective.'

Her version was confirmed by talks with individual children: with Lucy who had a three day's journey before she reached her home in Oriente; with two little sisters whose father was a cane cutter; with an eleven-year-old whose widowed mother worked in a people's store, and with an eighteen-year-old who had been at school here since she was eleven and on graduation was going to return home to teach in her own countryside.

As was often the case while I was in Cuba, I found the absence of strain that comes from individual competition which here is replaced by a sense of belonging to a group by whom you as an individual are needed and to whose progress you contribute by developing your capabilities. Very much is demanded of young people in Cuba and there may well be other strains difficult to detect in so short a time, but these children had the poise and uninhibited friendliness of children who feel secure in their world.

From what I could observe, the relationship between the girls and their young teacher was close and affectionate and they appeared to look upon her as a friend. Throughout our talk, the girls linked arms with her and I imagine her approval was important to them. However, approval by the group was clearly the main incentive for socially acceptable behaviour like keeping one's room and clothes tidy, or working and studying hard to help one's country. Clearly too there was inducement for the individual child to fit in with the ideals of the group which themselves were modelled by the ideals set by society as a whole and personified in such national heroes as José Martí and Antonio Maceo and Che Guevara.

Co-education is general policy in Cuba and the Ana Betancourt schools are the exception in being one sex schools. I wondered how far this situation was offset by other factors. All the managers I met were women. Of the three teachers I saw two were men and visiting specialists included both men and women. I was told that the younger girls joined Pioneer Clubs in the area and the older girls mixed with the opposite sex in other youth organisations. Some teaching practice is also carried out in mixed schools in the area. Added to this a variety of mass organisations 'support' the schools and partially take the place of uncles, aunts and grandparents.

It seemed to me that in some cases it must require a strong sense of duty (revolutionary conscience as the Cubans would put it) for girls who had grown used to community life in Havana to return and teach in their country homelands. I was told that these problems had sometimes arisen but in any case, now that purpose-built schools were becoming available, future educational development lay in co-educational boarding schools and teacher training colleges in each region where the pupils lived. The Ana Betancourt project had served its purpose and served it outstandingly well but now that many divisions between town and country were disappearing, it would be brought to a close as soon as purpose-built schools become available. So I was indeed fortunate to have had the opportunity to see something of this historic experiment before it ended.

As we left, I noticed two girls on the balcony in militia uniform. The housemother explained: 'Girls from fourteen years onwards join the Youth Militia. The object is twofold: to develop a sense of responsibility and patriotism, and to protect their dormitories.' Guard duty begins at an early age in Cuba since the never forgotten invasion of 1961. The youth slogan is *Work, Study, Defence.*

TABLE TALK

IT WAS evening before we once more viewed the sea and the twenty stories of the Hotel Habana Riviera, graceful structure of glass and concrete built by the Americans some thirty years ago. That night, as the sky outside darkened and lights glanced back from mirrored walls, we ended a rewarding day with a long conversation over a leisurely meal. Much on the menu was new to me as, for instance, the fine flavoured fish of tropical waters. Traditionally Cubans have eaten little of this valuable source of protein but now that the increase in Cuba's fishing fleet and in her catch is one of the best success stories of the revolution, there has been a campaign to eat more fish and it now appears regularly on most menus. Meat on the contrary has been in short supply but the frog legs on the menu made a good substitute for young chicken. Havana is now surrounded by a green belt with orchards of citrus fruit and tomatoes, vegetables and dairy produce all of which is now more freely available but at the time, because of transport and refrigeration problems, fruit and green vegetables were very scarce, so that the guava juice was a special treat. So also was the excellent small cup of Cuban coffee and my first introduction to a *daiquiri* – the famous drink topped with superb Havana ice cream which was supposed to have been concocted for Hemingway as a delicious way of keeping his weight down. (Hemingway's beautiful home in Havana Province which his wife donated to the Cuban nation remains just as he left it, hunting trophies and all.)

Fair shares

The Cuban tradition of generous and courteous hospitality

78

has little to do with the desire to impress. It was explained to me that the deep seated custom of every family is to give of its best to a guest whatever the sacrifice. Such hospitality is easy to abuse and in 1971 I was very conscious of the fact that I was in Cuba at a time of great scarcity of raw materials and consumer goods when everything was rationed as the most just way of distribution. Rationing remains today but supplies have considerably increased. Milk for instance that had almost disappeared from the menu of adults now allows for a pint a day for all children under seven, a special ration for over sixty-fives and an increasing amount of tinned milk for each family unit with extra for families of five and over. Eggs, too, are much more plentiful with some available off ration. Beef remains scarce but is supplemented by pork and chicken while fish is off the ration altogether, and butter, too, is growing more plentiful.

Returning to Cuba, the most noticeable change in two years was the vegetable booths in Havana stacked with green bananas, celery, roots and lettuce with locally canned tins of beans obtainable off ration on the shelves. Yoghourt and cold milk are on sale at ice cream bars. One saw shoppers at times with pineapples in their arms but while plentiful in the countryside, fruit was hard to obtain still in Havana, though refrigerators, on show in the shops, must be gradually easing the storage problems. Electrical goods such as refrigerators and washing machines are allocated through work centres with priority given to working women. The boot and shoe shortage seems to have been solved. As for all essential goods, the basic ration remains but more varied styles at a higher price are on display in shops on the free market. All the main stores now show a small selection of goods off ration, mainly non-essentials like cosmetics, cameras, gramophone records, jewellery but also some household goods and items of clothing. The idea is that extra money earned, for instance, by those doing plus-work (the emphasis is now on payment to each according to his or her work contribution) can be spent on these extras if desired and a black market avoided.

But, as Monica pointed out, even in 1971 a list of rations meant very little because the basic ration was supplemented by canteen meals served free in an increasing number of schools and cheaply at places of work. Many pre-school age children in day nurseries received a midday and an evening meal as well as extra milk and juice. In cooperation with the World Food and Agricultural Organisation, the diet and canteen system in the nursery groups throughout Cuba and workers' canteens in Havana had been overhauled with a view to providing as balanced a diet as possible in conditions of scarcity. The platter of food I saw served in a secondary school for a main meal contained a rice dish made with meat and egg, root vegetables, cooking bananas, something that looked like blancmange for a sweet and a drink of fruit juice.

Conversation and a meal at a restaurant is obviously a popular way of spending free time and family parties of Cuban workers gather in Havana's elegant eating places and the former exclusive restaurants housed often in houses of historic beauty. Eating out has become much more easily accessible in the last few years with less need to queue. Incidentally I was interested to see that most shops had special arrangements by which women workers could leave their baskets and I noticed some husbands and sons among the shoppers. There were also notices in shop windows stating that priority in serving would be given to women working in agriculture during the periodic distribution of dress materials, shoes and other rationed goods, and I understand that what is known as the Plan Jaba has extended this right to nearly fourteen thousand women workers.

I met no one in Cuba who tried to blame all shortages and setbacks on the American blockade. My Cuban hosts frankly admitted that inexperienced people suddenly finding themselves in complex positions of responsibility made mistakes. Like the coffee that was planted in Havana Province without proper soil tests and the rushed order of refrigerated trucks for which a special effort had been made only to find that due to language difficulties and insufficient care the gauge had been wrongly checked. Part of the evil effects of semi-colonisation was that the know-how was mostly imported from the United States so that too few Cubans were involved in the over-all management of industry, and a sizeable proportion of those who were, left the country when the Americans departed. Many businesses were branches of large US concerns like American Nestlè, General Motors and United Fruit. Some I was told were literally run by remote control: when there was a breakdown, management rang up head office in the USA and if necessary a plane would arrive with specialists and technicians. Then suddenly all this stopped and not even spare parts were available. When experts from the socialist countries came to the rescue, it was not just a matter of transporting everything from many thousand miles away but a great deal of complicated adjustments had to be made on both sides.

Cuban leaders have said that without the support of the socialist world they could not have survived. At the same time they stress the fraternal basis of aid within the planned economy grouping of COMECON (the nearest equivalent to the Common Market). This 'partnership of equals' theme was emphasised during an informal interview I had at the Ministry of Foreign Affairs, in relation to the sensitive question of the missile crisis of October 1962 – a period that, despite the absence of all panic, must have been as traumatic for Cuba as for the rest of the world. After the Bay of Pigs incident it seemed certain that a full scale American attack would follow. From whichever side the suggestion came of bringing Soviet missiles to Cuba as a deterrent, I was told one could be quite certain that they would not have arrived without Cuban approval since relationships had always been as between sovereign and equal partners. Luckily sanity prevailed when, after direct confrontation between Kennedy and Kruschev, the missiles were withdrawn and a promise given that there would be no future invasion of Cuba. In fact, twelve years have passed without invasion, in which Cuba has been able to consolidate her socialist state.

'There are no little blacks, nor little whites – only Cubans.' Antonio Maceo.

An added pleasure at mealtimes was the presence in the dining-room of young Cuban couples of whom there was always a sprinkling among the hotel's more usual clientele of foreign technicians and visitors. The capacious changing rooms on the balconies surrounding the swimming pool have been converted to chalets for these 'honeymooners' and though their price is probably high, young workers are obviously able to afford them. It is also obvious that in Cuba today pairing is between all shades of colour.

There has been since colonial times a large proportion of Cubans who were descendants of mixed alliances but these tended to be consensual rather than legal marriages where the norm imposed by society was that like should marry with like. In her examination of elopement in relation to marriage, race and class in nineteenth-century Cuba (*Revista de la Bibleoteca Nacional José Martí* May/August 1971) Vera Martinez Alier uses court evidence to show that the primary criterion of social classification was race with such questions as occupation, wealth and sexual respectability affecting this basic difference. That race was the main dividing line in nineteenth-century Cuban society is proved by the existence of special legislation regulating and restricting interracial marriages. The writer points out that antagonism to 'people of colour' on which it was based was not antagonism to colour as such but to colour as an indicator of relationship to slavery, for the civic power regarded slave status and therefore African origin, as a stain that contaminated a slave's descendants. The state's hierarchical views of racial purity were not in theory shared by the Catholic Church which took the view that all Catholics were equal and therefore free to intermarry, but the civic law was paramount.

Special licences were required throughout most of the nineteenth century for those wishing to marry across the colour bar. Young people who defied the dictates of their elders in these matters could appeal to the law against their parents' refusal to give permission or they could force their hand by eloping, in which case, because of the high value placed on the virginity of the girl, fear of dishonour for the family often caused the parents to reconsider their opposition to an 'unequal' marriage provided the inequality was not too great. Except for a brief period during the Ten Years War, in 1868 when the revolutionary government introduced absolute freedom of civil marriage for all over eighteen years in the limited territory under its control, it was not until after 1881 that a civil decree was passed granting freedom of marriage between races in Cuba. Long after that, racial and class prejudice tended to enforce the old standards but increasingly the fight for national independence was identified with the fight for racial equality.

At dinner one evening I turned the conversation to the general question of racial equality in Cuba, a question about which I am not, from any point of view, qualified to form an opinion. I was reminded that Cuban culture owes its rich complexity to both its African and its Spanish inheritance and, very important for its effect on children, outstanding heroes in Cuban history were black and of mixed race as well as white. In 1959, soon after the overthrow of Batista, Fidel Castro on behalf of the Council of Ministers spoke on 'the Rights of the Black Man in Cuba', and announced a campaign to end discrimination 'particularly in the working centres . . . where in some centres there has existed a shameful proceeding of excluding black people from work.' Conflict along racial lines was outlawed in Cuba. Equality of opportunity is official policy in schools, in places of work and all aspects of social life. Of course with slavery not more than ninety odd years ago, prejudice of the mind is not wiped out overnight but my Cuban friends felt that working, playing and growing up together in the new boarding schools was speeding up the successful building of a truly multi-racial state.

In this connection it is interesting to see how the question of race was treated in a manual prepared for the use of volunteer teachers during the drive to end illiteracy in the early years of revolutionary rule (1961). The passage to be studied is headed by the words of José Martí. 'To be a human being, is to be more than white, more than black, more than a mixture of both,' and it reads.

Racial discrimination always has an economic base. The exploiting countries in order to justify the way they exploit other peoples, label them as inferior races and therefore without the right to liberty and the full dignity of man.

There is no rational basis for racial discrimination. Science has demonstrated that all men are equal, that there are no essential differences between white men, black men or people of the yellow races. The structure of skin and bones, the composition of the blood, the functioning of bodily organs and the intelligence is similar in all people. External differences like the colour of the skin, the shape of the nose and texture of hair are due to adaptations over the years to different types of climate. Since science has shown that in all these ways there are no differences between the races, there is no basis for race hatred least of all among Cubans.

Cuban people have been formed from diverse ethnic groups. On the one hand the whites, descendants of the Spanish who conquered and colonised our country; on the other hand the blacks who were brought from Africa to be used as slaves. Slavery led the colonisers to treat a slave as inferior except in one particular sphere. It was this exception that led to the two basic groups in our population becoming mixed over the course of centuries, so producing the mixture of black and white that can be considered the type most characteristic of our people.

Cuban people have always been united in our struggle for liberty and independence, where black and white fought together . . . Cubans must never forget that fighting side by side were Martí and Maceo, Guillermo Moncado and Calixta Garcia, Fidel Castro and Juan Almeida . . .

I was able to learn first hand how these principles worked out in the life of Pedro Pérez Sarduy with whose family and friends I spent most of my free time in the spring of 1975. By profession he works as a journalist in the Cuban Institute of Radiodiffusion. He is also one of Cuba's younger writers whose distinction as a poet was awarded first mention by the Casa de las Americas for his book of poems, *Surrealidad*. In 1969 he married an English history graduate and they have one son. At present Pedro is working on a book about domestic servants based on the pre-revolutionary experiences of his mother. She lives in Havana in a little alley of one room houses which share an outdoor pump, a shower and a toilet. Pots of green plants grown for medicinal and culinary purposes as well as for pleasure cluster at the entrance to her home. Here we talked one evening over a memorable meal of traditional Cuban food. rice with roasted red peppers, black beans in rich sauce, yucca like creamy marrow, and succulent chicken, pot roasted slowly over a charcoal fire which our hostess cooks on by preference, followed by mangoes and melons and piping hot sweet coffee. Accompanied by good Cuban beer and the songs of a guitar-playing uncle, it was an evening to remember, not least for the deep pride of the mother in the achievements of her son.

Pedro Ramón Pérez Sarduy was born in May 1943 in Santa Clara which he describes as one of the most racist towns of Las Villas Province. When he was eight years old his parents were divorced and for the next four years he and his younger sister were brought up in a small country town whose atmosphere he remembers as 'unbelievably hostile'. His father remained in Santa Clara scraping together a living as a shoemaker while his mother went to work as a housemaid in Havana in order to earn something for her own and her children's keep. Pedro has written vividly about this period of his life in a short piece entitled 'Siete Tiempos Muertos'* and, since his was the life of many children of poor

* 'Dead season' after the *zafra* when thousands of seasonal workers had no work or money.

85

black families, he has allowed me to quote from it.

There was a time, a 'dead time', when at mid-day I'd go down to Horacio's to buy a *negrito atropellao* (a sort of sandwich of cake-like bread with the sweet solid paste made of dark brown fruit). Then I'd go off with the bundles of watercresses I had to sell, sell so that next day when Grandpa paid a kilo (one centavo) for every bundle sold, I could eat at noon my *negrito atropellao*.

When it rained the boys' room, as Aunt Nena used to call it, would be very wet; it had a zinc roof which Tiballa had bought in the last *zafra* (the floor was still earthern) and I would listen close to the big drops falling heavily, wanting to be one of those drops myself and, when the sun came out above the mango tree, to turn into steam and evaporate away...

When it was *zafra* time at the sugar mill, Tiballa would go off in the early morning and wouldn't be back till late afternoon. Then he would get an idea in his head to get out his heavy old 'vaquetumbo' sandals and go off to his vegetable garden. 'Ramoncito ... Ramoncito, get to the pump and bring two buckets of water.' And so Ramoncito went to the pump and brought water again and again. There were times when the weight of the buckets nailed my eyes to the path I had beaten from the house to the pump. My eyes watered from the dirt, thinking that instead of a path it was an endless ravine.

One Sunday afternoon, one of those Sundays full of *guasasas* [small biting insects], I hadn't gone down town because I didn't have any shoes. So, washed clean by the shower, I stayed in the porch reading, for the hundredth time, the same comic. Then all of a sudden, like when the *guije** announces some good or bad omen, I heard a whistle which I hadn't heard for years, which made me realise that round the corner, by the big porched house of Pastora, the fat old woman who sold wonderful fruit-flavoured ice-cubes for a kilo, Papi was coming laden with parcels. I laughed, cried, even shouted as I used to before, and couldn't stop babbling.

* Cuban name for a goblin in Yoruba legend.

Afterwards we went out with my little sister who called Papi by the formal 'usted'. I told him about everything, but everything and he said, 'Stop your crying. Tomorrow we'll go away together.' At that time my sister was very little and I remember that 13th of May was my eleventh birthday.

When the writer was fifteen, his father took him back permanently with him to Santa Clara and did all in his power to give his son the education he never had himself. Sarduy describes the troubled times of the 'fifties.

The stench of oppression hung over the city of my birth. I began to study in high school; strikes followed one after the other almost continuously. My father, a shoemaker, earned just enough to give to 'Mama', my grandmother, what was necessary for me not to go hungry. But I worked too, or rather I was exploited. I earned a few cents at different jobs. laundry boy, shoemaker's assistant, painter; I counted the money for the *bolita*, a gambling game that my godmother-aunt ran, and one of my uncles would soon give me some money to take the lunch which Mama prepared for him to 'Majana', a whorehouse of which he was the owner no less.

To get to the *ballu* or whorehouse, I had to go through Santa Clara Leoncio Vidal Park. Along one side was the old Institute of Secondary Education (now pre-university) where I studied for my baccalaureate and took part in students' strikes. The park I mentioned was divided ... that is to say segregated. Those provincial parks function as the kind of 'place-where-one-always-has-to-go'; it's a social centre where even the briefest encounters take place. The inner part of the park had a circular path 'for whites only' and outer part, structured the same, 'for the coloured people'; in both places the logic was to stroll round and round, whiling away the hour as if on a carousel which had lost control – especially on Sunday evenings.

But now and then the bombs would explode in some part of the city. it was the urban guerrillas and their sabotage actions. In those years those whites who were pro-Batista used to say that when the *barbados* (bearded ones) came down from the hills they were going to put all blacks in a boat and let them sink, their ankles tied, to the bottom of the sea. But the first of January 1959 came. And one Spring day the people got tired and with an unruly bearded rebel leading the crowd we began to tear up that park with mallets, pick axes, with our nails even. The rage and the sun were such that it was difficult to control anger.

In July that same year, I took part in the Marathon of Freedom, flaming torch carried the length of the Island by dozens of runners from all provinces, a marathon which had set out from the cradle of the Revolution, Oriente, at the beginning of the month and was to end on the eve of the 26th in the Sports City of Havana. It was fantastic to see the big city again. But, there still remained some institutions with a certain segregationalist character. let us say tourism. After the event, we went to the then Havana Hilton where we were to sleep. They didn't want to let us in. ninety-nine per cent of the athletes and sports directors were black. Once again our handsome rebel* with flowing hair and wild beard intervened. After two hours and the great scandal created, we could rest.

In 1962, I had a grant to study poetry for some six months, stay in the same hotel, but now it belonged to the Revolutionary Government and was called Habana Libre. Afterwards I went back to Santa Clara to carry out my duties as Literary Assessor, duties which had been set in the scholarship contract for the course I had taken. My work consisted in encouraging amateur talent in creative literature.

But the province was still the province and I decided to return and stay in Havana for good. I continued my studies – begun in the Central University of Las Villas – in the School of Letters of the Faculty of Humanities at the University of Havana. 'Unproductive studies', my father used to say, who, after the Revolution and at the age of forty, began to study to become a metallurgical engineer and finished with great success. I became the

*A reference to Camilo Cienfuegos.

88

first black male Cuban to study in the School, although it had only recently opened as such. There was one other black student – a woman and a student from one of the African countries.

Many years have gone by – though not so many really – and now the schools of this island form a rainbow over the countryside as well as over the cities, where children, adolescents and adults can study. My son Ilmi who as yet is only a few months old, was born of the union of two different races and cultures, but born in this capital of friendship and solidarity. Although fourteen – even twenty – years are nothing in comparison with the prejudice unloaded on the West Indies with the slaves brought in by those first black cargoes, Ilmi and other children like him will not have to grow up as I did, in a society pregnant with undistilled corruption, a society which promoted as one of its coarsest values that of 'being white is a profession'.

Brief encounter

It was while reading a newspaper waiting for a meal in the hotel lounge towards the end of my first visit that I was approached by the only young person I met who was hostile to revolutionary Cuba. He was a seventeen-year-old electricity student who said. 'You are English and I have learnt English and I like England. In England you cut off your king's head when he abolished parliament. My parents were in a good business and used to own their own house. Don't believe all you read in *Granma.* You should talk to people in their houses. One day those who left Cuba will come back and change things.' I told him I had indeed spoken to people in their homes. I was sorry he was unhappy but many people had told me that though life was still hard, things were much more just and life more dignified since there was work for all. I also said that if he came to England he would see that we too had our housing and other problems. When I mentioned this conversation to my hosts they said that while the

89

great majority of students identified completely with the revolution, some – a comparative few – did not and I had met with an extreme case. This was also part of the reality of Cuba.

RECOLLECTIONS OF THE LITERACY CAMPAIGN

BREAKING DOWN of barriers between Havana and the countryside continued in 1961 (the Year of Education) during the historic campaign to end illiteracy when a quarter of a million Cubans including fifty thousand trained teachers, many thousand volunteer 'people's teachers' and ten thousand young people responded to the appeal. 'Let those who know more teach those who know less.'

A small museum in Havana tells the whole carefully documented story. Official figures showed that less than one in five Cubans could read or write and 800,000 children were without schools, mostly in isolated country areas. Many of the volunteer *alphabetores* left the cities for the first time to live for a period with the farming people, share their work and teach the family, grandparents included, the rudiments of reading and writing. As proof that they had reached a minimum literacy, learners took a simple reading test and wrote a letter to Fidel Castro, letters that can still be read in a file in the museum today. In one year's crash programme, illiteracy, given in the 1953 census as 22.1%* for Cubans over fifteen years old (double in country areas), dropped to 3.9% – a fact later investigated by UNESCO and described as probably unequalled in the history of education.

It was Eva who gave me insight into the value of the experience for the youngsters who volunteered to teach, one third of whom were under fifteen years old. Eva is a twenty-five-year-old Cuban of African descent who worked as a designer for Cuban Tobacco. I was introduced to her by an English friend during the eerie days when Cyclone Laura was hanging about the Caribbean. Outside the brilliance of

---

* The higher figure of 23.6% illiteracy in 1958 occurs in Cuban sources, perhaps calculated from a younger starting age.

earth and sky had been transformed into the total grey of ceaseless rain, and storm shutters at the hotel windows enclosed us in a strange twilight world. Even though the hurricane luckily did not spend its force on Havana, the sea was leaping over the sea wall and washing right over the esplanade. I remember our meeting particularly because news had just come over the television screen that in the neighbouring province of Pinar del Río ninety-five per cent of the young tobacco seedlings had been damaged and hundreds of volunteers were mobilising to replant when this became possible. Cuba had learnt from the devastation caused some years previously by Hurricane Flora and twenty-six thousand people had been evacuated as a precaution but the only human victim reported was a thirty-four-year-old man trying to cross the river.

Pinar del Río (Pines by the River) was the province to which Eva was assigned during the literacy campaign. Becoming a *brigadista* had obviously been a turning point in her life and her memories poured out faster than I could write them down.

Before I joined the brigade, I took part in the illiteracy census at the end of 1960. I was fourteen years old and at the time belonged to Socialist Youth. Our job was to detect children who were not at school as well as make a list of older people who could not read or write. I was so dismayed by the degree of illiteracy that I wanted to go on doing this sort of work. Then there came the appeal for volunteers to go to the countryside and teach and I longed to go but no young person was accepted unless they had their parents' signature giving consent. My mother was a member of the old Communist Party and had been active in the underground movement in Batista's day, so she well understood the needs of the Revolution. At the same time, having lost my father, she could not bear to see the family separated particularly my sister and myself. So it was a great conflict for her. But I argued with her and when she saw how serious I was, she gave in. Where parents were less committed, permission was sometimes refused because rumours were spread that the Revolution wanted to take young people away and brainwash them.

Enrolment was followed by a week's intensive course for which we were taken in bus loads to Veradero, where boys and girls camped separately. I still remember my wonderful first sight of the sea. Here we were shown films and generally prepared for what was to come. A pilot group who had already been teaching coached us in teaching methods and led discussions on the relevance of the campaign for the success of the Revolution. I remember I was very proud to belong to the Brigade Conrado Benítez, in the first brigade to be formed from secondary school kids. [Conrado Benítez was the name of a young black teacher killed in the mountains by counter revolutionaries.] Then we were given two sets of uniform. green militia trousers, grey shirt, boots, green beret, epaulettes with the badge of the brigade and a rucksack containing three notebooks, a basic reader and a teaching manual. Finally with a paraffin lantern, fruit juice and food we were equipped for the journey.

I was disappointed at first when I heard that my group, half girls and half boys, was being sent to the westernmost province of Pinar del Río because like everyone else I had hoped for the Sierra Maestra but when we arrived at the end of the journey and my name was called to go into the hills of Pinar del Río I no longer minded. Next day we were taken a whole day's journey to the peasants' houses where we were to stay. This was my first glimpse of real country and I could not take my eyes off the strange landscape of the province with the fertile valleys and curious rock formations. I was not at all frightened but exhausted and longing to get to my host's house and see what it was all like.

Eva knew of course that she was not alone, that she would be working in close touch with others of her group and with their tutor, a trained teacher. Indeed in each region there was someone whose special job it was to act as liaison between peasant families and their new guests and sort out the domestic problems that were bound to arise. Nevertheless a little apprehension must have been mixed with the excitement when this fourteen-year-old black girl from the city approached the dwelling where she was to live. It was a wooden *bohío*, one of the better ones with a concrete floor, palm flank walls and palm-leaved-thatched roof. From the beginning she was overwhelmed by the kindness and hospitality of those who were waiting to greet her – a peasant family of Spanish extraction. There was much that was strange. the mice in the roof at night, no electricity, no sanitation at all, water from the river and unaccustomed foods, but soon she got used to it all, loving the wooded country with the lush flowering trees, the bathes in the river and the journeys on horseback to the house of the group tutor. She worked with the family and neighbours during the day and in the evening taught them the rudiments of reading and writing. At first she was nervous, but when she found her grown-up pupils were keen to learn and even put aside tasks to do so, she gained confidence. She in her turn learnt many practical things in the house and in the tobacco fields that were entirely new to her and stood her in good stead in later years. Her mother, who came on a three days' visit during the rains when the river broke its bank, was delighted to find her skinny little daughter had put on fourteen kilos in three months.

At weekends, Eva's group met together centrally to exchange experiences and attend study circles. She remembered visiting a house in which her friend was staying where an old peasant woman dominated her large family. Her great pride was her youngest son who had reached sixth grade in his education and was studying to become a tractor driver. Another son in the Rebel Army was an equal source of pride. The rest of the family worked in tobacco, selecting the leaves of a fine sort of tobacco that is grown in these parts on small plantations. In all these visits the young brigadistas experienced the great hospitality of the farming people.

There was much talk in the evenings about the subject

matter of the reading primer and about life in the new Cuba. The teaching manual *Alfabeticimos* used by the volunteer teachers is described in the introduction as 'a guide to a series of themes which simply and concretely discuss some fundamental questions concerning the process of our Revolution'. Headings of these themes include. the Revolution, Fidel is our Leader, the earth is ours, the cooperatives, nationalisation, friends and enemies, Imperialism, workers and peasants, war and peace, international unity, freedom of belief, industrialisation. Volunteers are advised to avoid all tone of authority and giving orders 'remembering that the task can only be achieved by the joint effort of both *alfabetizador* and *alfabeto*'.

Not even the Bay of Pigs invasion of Cuba in April 1961 halted the campaign against illiteracy in Cuba, which besides reducing the percentage of those who could neither read nor write, was also an intensive political exercise to educate people in the beliefs of the revolution. The end of the campaign was celebrated in a gathering of all who took part in Revolution Square to hear Fidel Castro speak on December 22nd 1961. Eva remembered the vast square jammed full of people and the emotional atmosphere as they heard him declare Cuba free of the drawback of illiteracy. All brigadistas were given the opportunity of scholarships with full board to study for a certificate of education. She herself began training but later transferred to a design course and today at twenty-five still feels the benefit of her stay with the farming people in her work for Cuba Tobacco. 'Perhaps not all experiences were as fortunate as my first one but I do know that I am only one of thousands for whom being a brigadista was an emancipation from home and a widening of horizons. It helped us to grow up,' she said.

SCHOOLING THE WHOLE MAN—
CUBA'S EDUCATIONAL REVOLUTION

THE TEN years following the literacy campaign saw intensive efforts to strengthen the learning habit by involving those who had taken part in mass adult education, this time with the new aim of every Cuban citizen achieving at least sixth grade level of primary education. Continuation classes were organised in three systems, regular, mountain and rural and in classes held at work places and in family circles, half a million adults (586,000) returned to school to wage 'the battle for the sixth grade'. Now, in the 'seventies, through what is known as the Parallel System of Education or Permanent Education one gets the impression that every other person one meets in Cuba from hotel staff to housewives, farmers, soldiers, factory workers, fishermen is attending classes. The current slogan is *'every worker a student – every student a worker'*. According to a report to the Eighteenth Pan-American Conference in 1970 nearly eight thousand were enrolled in worker-farmer educational programmes in preparation for university courses, a figure which had increased considerably by 1973 when one out of three people in Cuba were attending classes of some kind, with the total of all students in that year reaching 2,690,000 as compared with 811,000 in 1958-59. In 1974-75 about thirty-five thousand workers were attending various courses arranged by the Ministry of Education.*

An outstanding feature of what the Cubans call their educational revolution is the combination of education, study and work. I was able to get a close up view of how this principle worked in two junior secondary schools of a type which is being repeated throughout Cuba.

*However in a national census of education now being undertaken by the CTC (the Central Organisation of Cuban Trade Unions) preliminary results show that there are still 734,204 workers with less than a sixth-grade education.

The island's fertile soil shows red between the rows of young lemon trees which form part of an extensive citrus plantation near the town of Ceiba del Agua, in the province of Havana. Here several hundred acres of fruit, pineapple and coffee are tended and harvested by the pupils of one of the new 'Schools in the Countryside' (Secondaria Básica en el Campo) – an educational project that plans over the next decade to transfer all secondary schools to weekly boarding schools built to a similar design and strategically placed in the countryside (Plate XI).

'Beware of producing a human being with an outsize head and tiny hands,' wrote José Martí, Cuba's philosopher-poet and national hero of the last century's independence struggles. This latest development in Cuba's educational revolution is trying to provide a way of living that gives 'the whole man' a chance to develop. It also aims to meet the country's urgent need for increased food production.

Ceiba 1 was the first of nine schools to be built in this section of the green belt south of Havana. The peace of the place on the day of my visit made it hard to believe that the pleasant prefabricated buildings interlinked by covered ways house two hundred and fifty girls and two hundred and fifty boys. A recent heavy tropical shower had temporarily waterlogged the land so the specially built small tractors were not in use but boys and girls were at work in the lemon groves and in the classrooms, or playing chess, or practising a song in the sun for Che Guevara's anniversary. By mistake no notice had been given of my visit so I was seeing a normal day.

Cuba by policy and of necessity entrusts its young people with great responsibility. Because of the composition of its nearly ten million people less than a third of the population is of normal working age and there was still in the early 'seventies an acute shortage of trained people.

The director of this countryside school of five hundred pupils was at the time of my visit a young man of twenty.

Until recently, the head master explained, all secondary schools used to move into camps in the countryside for up to forty-five days each year. During the day they helped the farmers with their crops, studied the history, geography and economy of the region and in the evenings organised sports, music and drama with the local community.

'It was a great experience for the children and, on the whole, good for production since labour is short, but it interrupted the school schedule. This is why Fidel thought out a new kind of school which would be situated in the countryside and regularly combine productive work with normal school activity.'

Board, tuition, uniform and books in the new schools are free. There are well equipped laboratories and a theatre, so their cost is high, but they have been so planned that over a period each school will cover its own cost.

Five mornings a week pupils spend four hours in the classroom daily and three in the field, alternating in two shifts. 'We find already that the kids love the outdoor work: that physically they are better developed, class results have improved and there is a better attitude to work and responsibility,' the director told me.

Informal exchange of opinion with a group of young people at another school of this type near Jaguey Grande in the province of Matanzas confirmed the opinion that the life suited them mentally and physically. This was the First Congress School opened by Fidel Castro in April 1971 and named after Cuba's First Congress of Education and Culture.

While I was served school lunch in the dining room, a group of teachers and pupils answered questions. After a morning in the field (breakfast 6.15 and start work 7.30) wasn't everyone too exhausted to settle to class work? I was told it didn't work that way. The change prevented you getting stale and after the long two hour lunch and siesta break (12-2 p.m.) you were ready for class work. Results measured by examinations (much used in Cuba) prove the

98

point. The school academic schedule is the one used nationally and academic results, measured by numbers graduating from one grade to the next, in the new schools continue to remain well above average. Everyone was convinced that what Fidel Castro had said in his inauguration speech was being proved in practice: provided education in the widest sense was given top priority, there need be no contradiction between study and production. On the contrary each enriched the other. As a young biology teacher put it: she found book learning took on a new dimension for both teacher and pupil when what you learnt could be tested immediately out there in the plantation where it was linked with the needs of real life.

Would the interest in the field work last when the novelty had worn off? Yes, they argued because each brigade had its own particular lemon grove or other area to look after so that everyone could see the effect of their own work right through the year until harvest. Each brigade of twenty worked with a teacher-supervisor and elected a brigade leader. These two met weekly with the school production director to work out a target which each brigade member can be expected to reach in three hours. Apparently, much to the students' annoyance, the regional farm manager at first suggested only half the adult production norm, but when they got through this in about a third of the time it was raised to the adult worker's level. Some enthusiasts claimed it still was not high enough.

I sat in for half an hour at a mathematics lesson. One of the big changes in content and approach of Cuban education in 1969 was a switch over to modern mathematics. In an airy class room looking out on trees and equipped with television, thirty-five pupils of tenth grade (fifteen plus) were sitting in desks and rose to greet us. The teacher explained that the class would not be typical as he was running over a test and therefore would be talking more than usual. I was told the emphasis in tests was on the progress of the whole group rather than on individual competition.

History in the primary school concentrates mainly on

Cuban history, though one book used is about children in the Congo, Vietnam and Bolivia. The syllabus widens out to ancient and world history at the secondary stage with a final course then named 'Problems of the world today'. The approach is Marxist and aims to trace the evolution of life, showing the struggle and contradictions in all social systems and the developing role of the workers.

This school confirmed the impression gained at all types of school I visited: out of school activities organised since 1963 in circles of interest play an outstanding part in Cuban education. Emphasis in keeping with Cuba's needs as an underdeveloped country is scientific and technical with small groups following their interests in upkeep of machinery, printing, pollination experiments and bee keeping, astronomy, plant breeding and pest control. There was also the same wide choice of art clubs that I had seen in the Ana Betancourt schools, meeting one or two nights a week for those interested in painting, theatre, film literature, dance and music groups.

The school theatre at Jaguey Grande seats two hundred and fifty and the day I was there the Students' Federation was calling a meeting to discuss producing *Oedipus Rex*. Leadership of the Federation of Secondary School Students is elected by secret vote from nominations made by each class. Every class elects a class council while the full school council consists of representatives of the Federation, the Union of Young Communists, the teachers' union and the Communist Party. There is also a council of educational directors consisting entirely of teaching and administrative staff.

One of the declared aims of Cuban education is the formulation of a new twenty-first-century human being with different, less self centred attitudes to life and work. Slogans on the school notice board gave some idea of what is required: 'Consider the individual and the collective . . . Look after equipment . . . Attendance and punctuality.'

On my tour of the school I noticed both boys and girls were sweeping the dormitories. Everyone agreed that such sharing was only just, although traditionally this would have been a rare sight in most Cuban homes. The Spanish tradition of *machismo* looked upon such co-operation as a departure from masculinity and this attitude dies hard. In schools however, it obviously has no place in the formation of what Cubans call, quoting Che Guevara, the new type person for the new society.

Vocational schools

These matters formed part of a discussion I had with students of revolutionary Cuba's first vocational school, 'Vento Secondaria', whose formation in 1966 was inspired by a national display of the work done by the scientific Circles of Interest. Entry to these vocational schools is selective based on primary school results and a student's overall school record. Priority is given to those wishing to pursue scientific and technical careers where Cuba's need for qualified people is greatest and students are given every help in preparing for such careers including practical participation in the relevant industry.

The headmaster of Vento Secondaria called a group together at random from pupils passing the door of his study. Ages ranged from fourteen to fifteen and there happened to be only one girl in the group but perhaps this was representative as I was told that to date there had always been a large proportion of boys. Careers chosen by those present included mathematics, anthropology, electronics, nuclear physics and constructional engineering while outside interests were choral singing, painting, guitar playing, theatre and sports of all varieties. All belonged to the student union and all were very vocal, dealing with my questions as a group with obvious enjoyment.

I asked what they thought was the most important thing I should tell their English contemporaries about the Cuban Revolution. 'Explain,' said one of them, 'that we are trying to build a new society without imperialists,' and added another, 'because Cuba is not a rich country, this means everyone going all out to increase production in whatever way they are able.' I asked what they thought was meant by the phrase one often heard, 'New man for a new society'. Between them they built up a picture of what Cubans mean by this phrase: 'a revolutionary with a conscience like Che's . . . just, honest, one who never gives up when things get difficult . . . seeing work as more than just earning money in order to live . . . having a strong feeling for the collective and solidarity with others . . . being humane'. One of the younger boys said we ought to have begun with internationalism and he explained how various school groups had been working on projects about other countries. Visitors from near by Latin America and from Africa and Asia had been interviewed by students on life in their country, and they hoped to extend the friendships made.

Finally I asked what did they think could be done by everyone to help ensure that women and girls played an equal role with men at all levels in the community since Lenin had said that a socialist society could never be built without the full participation of women. Answers to this one were slower coming. One of the oldest boys replied that after the Revolution women had raised their political level and were increasingly taking part in production. 'What women are doing in Cuba is very good. Through the way they work in political organisations and in the Women's Federation as well as other organisations they have been a great help to the Revolution. As far as girls are concerned, in this school they have shown themselves to be revolutionaries because, while some might prefer to live at home, they realise that the new-type schools need both boys and girls for success and joining in a resident school community can give them real equality better than in the four walls of their own house.' When everyone looked at the girl student to speak, she said: 'To us it is a pride and satisfaction to be working always together with men because even though they are supposed to be strong, they can feel weak without our help. Women are important and they too have proved that they are prepared to defend their country to the death if need be.'

No one mentioned the question of equality in the home so I pointed out that while all this sounded beautiful in theory did they not agree that in practice it was impossible for women to play a full part unless all shared in helping in the home. What happened in their own homes? After some amusement tinged with embarrassment at the unexpected personal approach, a fifteen-year-old boy answered: 'You know, all this is improving. I have a friend who is a teacher, with a wife also a volunteer teacher. Both are communists and their children go to nursery school and I know for a fact that when she works he takes over the housework and shopping. They share the domestic work and this is becoming the fashion among younger people.' We none of us knew then that we were scratching the surface of a subject which later was to become matter for a great national debate and much heart searching.

Cuba's educational plans provide for seven new vocational schools with a total of twenty-five thousand pupils for which the Lenin School completed in 1974 will set a standard. Here provision for its four and a half thousand students includes science and language laboratories, amphitheatres with cinema screens, a closed circuit television network and a data processing centre where the computers used are assembled by the pupils. Linked with the work-study programme at this school is a workshop for the assembly of radios and a factory for turning out mini-computers which is being built with the aid of the socialist countries. Generous provision for arts activities would seem to suggest that these schools though strongly science orientated are in no way narrowly vocational. There are drama halls, music training rooms, art rooms and dance halls, while installations for sport, which is a Cuban passion, range from two Olympic swimming pools to racing tracks, fencing halls, baseball courts and five rooms for chess playing.

Standard of equipment is also good at Cuba's new poly-technic schools (entrance after sixth grade primary) and technical institutes (entrance after eighth and ninth grade). These are now being built next door to sugar mills, factories and farms where students spend four hours each day participating in production. A large electronics institute, for instance, has recently been built with the cooperation of the Swedish International Development Authority and UNESCO. It is located near a major plant for the manufacture of radio, television and electronics and equipment is said to be worth about a million dollars. High standards like these are only possible in a developing country like Cuba because of the policy of direct integration of all students into her programme of economic and social development and it is hoped by 1980 that Cuba's educational costs will be covered by the productive work of the students.

'That is how we want the children of our America to be: men who say what they think and say it well: sincere and eloquent men.' José Martí in *The Golden Age*, a book for children.

Cuban leaders increasingly emphasise the concept of collective responsibility but in talking to Cuban children one quite often hears the phrase 'Fidel thinks . . . ' as though referring to a near friend. At the same time Cuban children's ability to express and develop their own ideas is something that impresses most visitors. Relevant to this was an opinion passed by Cuban novelist and diplomat Lysandro Otero Gonzalez who has children of his own. He told me he believed in exposing young people to varying currents of thought as the best way of equipping them for what he called 'the battle of ideas'. He drew a parallel with the child who when kept in isolation from germs falls a victim to the first one that comes along but develops resistance if exposed to them. But he drew a firm distinction between this view point and 'liberalism' which gave no guide lines. Personally I hope that Cuba's faith in her young people will increasingly lead to educational methods that encourage them to think creatively and critically, saying what they think and saying it well, as Martí visualised.

I found the authorities modest about their educational achievements and anxious to give a balanced view. *Education,* a quarterly review published by the Ministry of Education, in its January-March issue of 1972 states that in rural Cuba primary school teachers have increased from 5,336 in 1958-59 to 24,501 in 1970-71 and primary school buildings from 4,889 to 12,583. (Many of these are single class schools but the growth remains notable.) After outlining the achievements of thirteen years the writer concludes by emphasising the lack of trained teachers and the need to improve the quality of teachers, textbooks and programmes. It was estimated that in the first five years of the 'seventies Cuba would need sixty-four thousand teachers and at the end of that time it is still far short of its needs.

On July 26th 1974 Fidel Castro added to this picture. He spoke of the needs piling up at the lower levels because while population was increasing at the rate of 200,000, school attendance of school age children had also increased to the extent that 98.5% of children were attending school compared with 56.4% in 1957. Drop outs too, which were high in the early years of the revolution, were down to 3%. The number of secondary school children had increased five times since the revolution and this, together with the country's need for skilled people, meant priority must be given to the building of secondary schools to meet the flood of boys and girls wishing to continue education beyond the sixth grade. This had meant, he said, that many teachers in primary schools as well as in the old secondary schools in Havana were working under conditions of strain. He knew, for instance, that some primary schools were housed in thatched cottages. The turn for new primary schools' building would come but meanwhile old buildings must be repaired and painted and a real concentration made on improving the number of teachers and the quality of books to tide over what he knew was a difficult period for those still working in the old schools.

105

I saw something of these conditions when I made friends with a large primary school in Havana. We first met casually at an army and navy day celebration when I found myself sitting on the sea wall next to a long row of small legs dangling over a considerable depth below. I was watching the quiet way a young male teacher was coping with their lively owners while a grandmother helper shared round a few refreshments. Before long they noticed me, our point of contact being a Free Angela Davis badge I was wearing. (At that time affection for the black American militant was at its height in Cuba.) Conversation opened, I was given my share of refreshments and when the purpose of my visit was authenticated by a young headmistress in militia uniform, I was invited to visit the school the following day.

An example of Cuban children's early introduction to some aspects of the world outside Cuba was a wall newspaper at the entrance to the school building with a large section devoted to black American Angela Davis and the campaign for her release from prison. I had not been in the kindergarten classroom for five year olds for more than a few minutes before a little monitor sprang to her feet and for my benefit conducted 'Song for Angela Davis', top of the pops in Cuba at the time. In this classroom there was room for movement but in others I visited the rooms were so jammed with desks that it was difficult to make one's way between them and in at least one case the only entrance and exit was through the next classroom. But the atmosphere seemed friendly and relaxed and despite language barriers I learnt a great deal from the teachers I met by the sea. They agreed with me that having seen Cuba's newest and best, it was good to see Cuba's oldest and worst since this also was part of Cuba's reality. (Incidentally I pointed out that Cuba was not the only one to have crowded classrooms.)

I later visited a country area primary school outside Havana. Named after one of Cuba's heroines, Tania the

Guerrilla, who was killed in Che Guevara's last Bolivian campaign (Plate I), the Haydée Tamara Bünke School was built by the revolutionary government to provide education for a dairy-farming area in Havana Province previously served by the one teacher for all grades schools. Buses collected children to arrive for breakfast at 7.30 (returning home at 4.30) from a scattered country area containing some five hundred farms and nine hundred families.

Attached to the school and serving the same area was a modern polyclinic with a maternity section. Before the Revolution less than twenty per cent of Cuban mothers had medical attention during birth. Nearly all mothers (ninety-five per cent) now have their babies in hospital and under the care of an obstetrician and it is significant that the maternal death rate has almost halved in twelve years to six deaths in ten thousand in 1972-73. Infant mortality figures are the lowest in Latin America and comparable to the developed countries at less than twenty-eight deaths for every thousand babies born live.

Increase in Cuba's birthrate is of moderate proportions. There seems to be no general national propaganda or campaigning concerning birth control but every polyclinic has its gynaecological section where advice and appliances are readily available. These consist mainly of the coil and the loop. The pill, largely for national economic reasons, is not used in Cuba.

Illegal abortion used to be one of the primary causes of maternal deaths. Now termination of pregnancy in hospital has helped to reduce deaths steeply. On my second visit to Cuba I discussed this matter with a young mother from Oriente now working in Havana. Decision concerning abortion, she said, is considered an individual matter for the pregnant woman. In exceptional cases when repeated abortions are likely to adversely affect the organs of reproduction, the local clinic makes proposals. A meeting is held with the couple where the dangers of repeated interruptions of pregnancy are explained and advice is given on birth control methods. If a woman has passed the recommended age for

107

childbirth or has a lot of children, she can ask for ligation but sterilisation is only carried out when the woman herself specifically requests it. As this young mother said, 'Parents know that in Cuba today there is good scope for the development of each child and generally speaking Cuban women want children.' (Nine in a family is not uncommon in Oriente where the birth rate is highest.) Cubans do not see the world's over-population so much as the cause of under-development as the result of underdevelopment. My Cuban friend was convinced that the birth rate would adjust itself with the cultural and social development of women and compared her own mother on a low income, who never became involved outside the narrow limits of the home, with a large family, and herself in salaried work of wide interest with one son.

No stigma of any sort is attached to children born out of marriage in Cuba. Paternity must be declared to ensure that the father assumes his share of responsibility and the un-married mother naturally has the same rights as any other. Since a new law of January 1974, Cuban women workers enjoy one of the most advanced maternity laws. Eighteen weeks maternity leave is granted with pay together with a further nine months leave without pay if the mother wishes to spend all her time with her child during this period, at the end of which time her job must remain open to her. A further day a month is also granted for visits to her own doctor and her child's with no loss of pay.

I noticed that in the children's wing of the clinic there was, besides the child's bed, a bed for the mother who could come into residence with the ill child. The clinic was mainly used for regular checking of the school children and their families, prevention of illness being the basis of Cuba's free medical health service, which, since 1973, has included a proportion of home visits to children and the elderly.

Half of all medical students are women as are sixty-two per cent of the Ministry of Health personnel. The student who showed us round was in her last year of medical train-ing after which she would practice in a rural area similar to this one. She spoke with enthusiasm of the Revolution's achievement in her own field, particularly in relation to contagious diseases, incidence of which had dropped to nearly two thirds in the last ten years. Partly because many medical students like her had volunteered for rural areas, there is a big change from 1958 when sixty-four per cent of Cuban doctors were in Havana. Today forty-two per cent are in the capital with the remainder spread over the rest of the island. Some of this information we obtained from the clinic dentist, an elderly black Cuban who I remember for his salutary sense of humour. He visited the clinic three days a week, attending each time to some twenty of his two thousand patients and beginning his dental care where possible with a photograph of the baby's mouth at forty-five days old.

Not far from the clinic and gleaming white against the green of the fields, classrooms ran round four sides of a quadrangle. The school, a pleasant single-storied building, was built in 1968 for two hundred and fifty children and three years later it housed four hundred so that all available space had to double up as teaching space, with lessons spilling over into the shaded areas outside on the day of my visit. Infants were singing an action song about how a baby must be cared for and my interpreter was impressed because the boys were joining in, rocking and caressing an imaginary doll in their arms, something which he said would have been frowned upon in his boyhood. For us they sang 'With Fidel to victory'.

The school day began with a fifteen minutes assembly when each class except the very young takes it in turn to read important news from the children's newspaper and give reports on daily attendance, on the activities of pioneer groups and on the results of class emulation. The headmistress, a gentle-voiced woman with two sons of her own, added that this also was a time for criticism of any little matter of discipline, but on the whole such problems were few. Corporal punishment is illegal in Cuban schools. Recently badges have been introduced in some secondary schools. Red ones are given to everyone on the first day of school and indicate vanguard pupils in matters of 'dedication, discipline, attitude to work and fighting spirit'. Some slip-up may mean having to substitute the red badge for a blue indicating a rather less than vanguard student or of course serious misdemeanour may mean loss of badge altogether! I saw none of these personal emulation badges while in Cuba, I am rather glad to say.

The science laboratory at the Tamara Bünke school contained three-dimensional models of a cow that could be taken apart for examination of the internal and reproductive organs. (There were similar human models of man and woman). A class was following a lesson on environmental studies, their ages ranging from twelve to fourteen owing to the fact that Cuban children remain in the same class until they pass the test for the next grade. While listening to the lesson I was invited to look at the students' folders containing the progress charts which are kept in some detail for all Cuban children. These together with regular examinations and a final diagnostic test are used to decide where a student should specialise when beginning a new course. The two essay subjects set for one such test were: What is a milk parlour and why does the Revolutionary Government seek to end the system of extensive grazing? What was the happiest day in your holiday? I was again told that emphasis in all tests is on the class as a whole reaching the required standard and with that end in view the group meets regularly to evaluate progress and organise extra help for those who need it.

Recent developments in Cuba's educational revolution

Cuba's contribution to UNESCO's World Education Report of 1971 refers to plans aimed at eliminating verbalism and learning by rote with 'a continuing fight to improve the quality of education and to make it more lively, dynamic and truly scientific'. I wondered if the national emphasis on grades and examinations and group emulation might not make the first of these aims harder to achieve and lead to cramming? Cuban teachers thought the individual class record helped to counterbalance this. However, an interesting recent development in this connection was described to me on my return to Cuba this year by Ana Maria, director of the People and Education Publishing House of the Book Institute who has a young son in the age group affected and is convinced that the change is of profound importance. The old grade system for grades 1 to 4 is to be abolished. At a stage in a child's life when development proceeds unevenly 'by leaps' as she put it, the grade system could be damaging for both child and teacher. It forced the child who could not pass the grade to repeat the year's work with children of a younger age so that sheer boredom sometimes produced problem children. It also encouraged teachers to take short cuts because they were judged on the numbers passing graduation tests. Under a new scheme tried out in Cuba for the past two years, for the first four years of primary school children will stay together as a group with the same teacher providing the continuity needed at this stage, and in these years assessment of progress will be by other methods than the formal examination.

'The teacher will have time,' said Ana Maria, 'to create the essential interaction between teacher and child, and get to know the actual problems of the children, building up confidence and helping them over the whole period to establish their identity while creating a true collective that will have four years to grow. By the end of the period, the children will be ready to pass to a further cycle of learning under specialist teachers for each subject. This new system is only one aspect of a thorough reorganisation aimed at transforming the quality and content of education so as to equip the new generation to solve the problems presented by our technical and scientific revolution. Legally, a child's education can at present end at sixth grade primary. However, we believe every child has the right to secondary and higher education and we recognise that this position cannot continue. The law has to remain as it is until we have created the material resources in the form of schools, teachers, equipment to make it possible to enforce a higher school leaving age, but by 1980-85 we hope that twelfth grade (about eighteen years) will be the compulsory attendance level in a work-study school programme. This will enable students to enter society adequately equipped without the over-heavy school schedules of the past.'

Ana Maria spoke too of the importance in this transition period of the polytechnical schools which will gather together young adolescents leaving the school system and those who have dropped behind, and offer them the chance of training as intermediate technicians. 'Backwardness', she said, 'affects the personality and we want to avoid producing men and women with psychological problems. Our research has shown that when they become involved in work and study that appeals to their more adult interests and makes them feel of use, young people find a way out of their previous difficulties and learn to read and apply themselves once they see a practical point in doing so.'

Cuba finds that the cure of many kinds of maladjustment in children lies in work and study group activity in the countryside. There are no penal institutions for children. Responsibility for bringing serious anti-social elements and children with personality problems back to society is shared between the neighbourhood Committee for the Defence of the Republic, parents, educationalists and psychiatrists.

More provision is planned for a section that is at present scantily provided for – handicapped children who require specialised education. Architects, medical men, and educationalists are meeting to design new schools to meet the needs of each type of handicap. Meanwhile a commission is studying the causes of handicap and certain types of abnormal births with special reference to social problems allied to interbreeding in isolated rural areas, problems to which, it is thought, a solution may be found in the new rural communities that allow of wider social development.

The veritable explosion in the numbers requiring secon-

112

dary and intermediate education together with the drive to improve the quality and content of educational books, has placed great responsibility on the People and Education Publishing House, but its lively young director obviously saw this as a challenge and was full of ideas on new ways to cope. She showed me, among other books, a first reading book introducing the child to simple concepts of the family, science, the homeland etc., on which she said some of Cuba's best brains had collaborated. There was also a book for the still existing all-age single-class small rural·school, carefully designed to allow children to read and study individually at their own pace and level.

A GRASS ROOTS ORGANISATION

EARLY EVENING in Havana is a time to be out of doors watching spectacular sunset skies changing over the sea, gold to amber, rose to purple, jade to indigo. A little inland after the day, the cooler air brings out the scent of the pines and then it is particularly pleasant to ramble the streets alone. The once fashionable area of Vedado is now lived in by Cuban workers. Here people go about their business or talk to neighbours sitting on Spanish rocking chairs outside the houses. In October the side streets are still filled with flowering shrubs and trees most bounteous in their size and colour, and now and again one finds chickens in front gardens or a goat nibbling the overgrowing weeds. One had to look out for pitfalls in the dark where pavements had fallen into disrepair but otherwise it seemed safe to wander alone in Havana any time of the day or night.

Part of the reason lies in a specifically Cuban phenomenon: the neighbourhood Committees for the Defence of the Revolution which exist in every street and apartment block. I ran across the local committee during one evening ramble when I noticed a mural in a front garden, lit by a lamp and covered with notices and colourful posters. All round the edge were small flags of Latin America. In one corner under a magazine photograph of José Martí was a press cutting reporting an attack, attributed to C.I.A. raiders, that same week on a coastal village in the east of Cuba which had resulted in the injury of two teenagers, one of whom had lost a leg. In the opposite corner in large print was the query *Have you been vaccinated?* The central poster typically made use of witty drawings with the sense of humour that is never very far below the surface in Cuba. The poster celebrated the anniversary of the Committees for the Defence of the

Revolution (CDRs) which it described as 'an organisation of the masses worthy of the hope that was placed in it'. Cartoon drawings illustrated the various jobs that a *cederista* (CDR member) was expected to tackle: being vigilant (with the typically Cuban light touch, this basic duty of revolutionary vigilance against enemy penetration was represented by a fun figure with the long nose of a nosey parker peering round a door), mending leaks in pipes, planting trees and sprucing up the neighbourhood, catching up on learning, showing international solidarity with Vietnam. Then there was a quote from Lenin in black and red: 'the most important factor, the decisive one for the triumph of the new regime is production', and pinned up beside it was a story for children from a Cuban magazine about a drone who would not work however hard the worker bees argued with him, but ate their food and grew fat until they chased him out of the hive to reform him (Plate XIV).

Seeing my interest in the mural, a passer-by pointed to the heavy raindrops now beginning to fall and rang at the door of the secretary's house for me. Soon the secretary, his wife and a neighbour who spoke English were exchanging information with me inside the shelter of the sitting-room.

Neighbourhood committees

Central to the Cuban style of revolution has been the way in which new expressions of people's participation have evolved and one of the most interesting of these are the Committees for the Defence of the Revolution. These CDRs came into being in the very first year after victory in 1960 when, in preparation for the Bay of Pigs invasion, a series of acts of sabotage were set in motion by those inside and outside Cuba who were opposed to the revolution. At a great assembly on September 28th 1960, Fidel Castro called upon the people to organise 'collective revolutionary vigilance'. My CDR friend remembers the electric atmosphere following the demonstration: 'I remember how we hung about long after

115

it ended planning far into the night what could be done. I forget where the idea of forming local defence committees started but soon they were being formed everywhere on a street and apartment block basis. Later it was all more organised and a national leadership was formed which linked up the regions.'

Testing time for the committees came early. When in 1961 invaders landed at the Bay of Pigs and called on the people of Cuba to rise and overthrow the revolutionary government, this people's defence organisation was already formed and, along with the militia, was largely responsible for preventing potential aid from within Cuba reaching the attackers. Vigilance is still seen as a vitally important function of the CDRs but their activities have now spread to many other aspects of civil life.

Today the membership has risen to four and a half million with membership almost equally divided between men and women and embracing eighty per cent of the population above the age of fourteen. One third of its members are in rural areas. When Dr Gutierrez Muniz, Minister of Public Health, reported that polio had been wiped out in Cuba, diphtheria reduced to two cases in three years compared with fourteen hundred cases in 1962, tetanus and tuberculosis in children greatly reduced and Cuba officially declared a malaria free country by the World Health Organisation, he specifically stressed that these results would have been unthinkable without the cooperation of the Cuban people's organisations, foremost among them the CDRs. They helped to vaccinate two million children against polio and their efforts to prevent waste and pollution, particularly important in an island desperately short of raw materials, include the collection of millions of bottles and about three thousand metric tons of used paper and cardboard for recycling. A lot of this energy today is being channelled into gardening and cleaning up the environment but in the early 'seventies one of the achievements that most caught the imagination of the committee members was the building of the fine Latin American stadium to the construction of which three hundred thousand Cubans gave a million hours of voluntary work. One begins to understand the frequent use of the word 'mass organisation' in Cuba!) The stadium was finished in time for the world baseball event in Havana in 1971 when it was jammed full of baseball fans many of whom had helped to build it (Plate I).

These committees provide a group of neighbours right on the doorstep who can be called upon to sort out any problem. They know the attitude of each tenant to the revolution, who attends school, who is available for voluntary work, who should receive attention from the social services and when help is needed they are able to mobilise the neighbours. There are probably some temperaments who would prefer to dispense with what they see as an intrusion into privacy but it is an interesting fact that in the large cities of the capitalist world people who feel overpowered by the growing distance between the governing and the governed are also turning to neighbourhood councils as a cure for loneliness and alienation.

Periodically, the CDRs call assemblies of all their members to consider the services in the area, and this is the opportunity to raise complaint against any institutions or individual. Any state or local government functionary so criticised is expected to attend a meeting to explain what steps have been taken to set things right. Not all take criticism well and as the national chairman of the CDRs pointed out, sometimes it requires quite a struggle to set things right.

A People's Court

At the time of my visit the neighbourhood committees were largely responsible for the People's Courts. These lower courts in the early 'seventies consisted of three lay judges elected by citizens on a neighbourhood basis who gave freely of their services during leisure hours. I was fortunate enough to attend a session of the People's Court in one district of

Havana. The proceedings were explained to me by a Cuban lawyer of Jamaican origin, an active member of the local committee and a spare time writer whom I met through a mutual friend. (A qualified lawyer attends the court in case the person whose misdemeanour is under discussion wishes to be represented but there is no paid bureaucracy in these lower courts which are handled by the local community.)

The CDR in this central district of Havana had good premises in what was once a bank, with seating for up to one hundred people. Already quite a crowd of people from the neighbourhood had arrived, among them a number of nine and ten year olds. Everyone is here, remarks my friend, everyone except the offender, though this was by no means unusual. Offenders had three opportunities to turn up at the court and if the third time they failed to come, they were transferred to a higher court. Finally Rosa, as we will call her, turns up – a handsome young woman with long side curls looking rather pale and tense. At a table were the three judges, a woman and two men. The chairman was at pains to point out to those present that the court was known as a consultative court because no verdict would be arrived at until everyone had had the opportunity to express his or her point of view, and moreover the consultative court was more interested in educating than in punishing. The visitors' request to be present was then put to the meeting with the explanation that we wished to see first hand the participation of the people in different aspects of life in Cuba, to which agreement was shown by handclapping. By now the room was packed with people and at 8.45 p.m. proceedings began.

The case against Rosa was brought by a young man known as the coordinator, on behalf of all members of the CDR. It centred round the unsatisfactory set-up in one of the people's shops and arose out of a previous court case in which assistants had been accused of holding back odds and ends for their friends – in conditions of rationing an anti-social offence. The chief offender had been sentenced to work on construction in the Lenin Park, residing there in a hostel for thirty days. (Not much of a punishment to work in a park, commented someone present.) One or two other shop assistants who were involved in a lesser way received a public rebuke and a caution.

Having explained the situation to date the coordinator stated that he had been asked to say that several CDR members on this occasion heard Rosa, as she left the court with others, being abusive about the proceedings and saying that people had better watch out. This was felt to be a serious slur on the court and on the people as a whole. The chairman asked the speaker to clarify certain points, requesting him to be more precise so that the whole court was clear what the charge was. Then the man from the Party spoke saying that at this time of great trials for the Cuban people this type of attitude and divisionary behaviour could not be tolerated.

It was now Rosa's turn to speak. Using the microphone she spoke briefly but fluently, pointing out that the last court case had gone on late into the night. She was tired out having left directly after work without a proper meal and she had spoken hastily because she was irritable and tired. She denied saying 'the people had better watch out' but apologised to the chairman for what had happened. The chairman in his turn said: 'I am only one of the court and you must direct your apologies to the whole court.' Then followed witnesses from the floor, mainly women who came forward to recount what they had heard said on the previous occasion. A student, who was Rosa's young man, spoke eloquently in her defence, underlining how exhausted she had been on the previous occasion while a neighbour pointed out that she had a good record for cooperating in voluntary work in which she was a reliable enthusiastic worker. Others added that in the shop she had a pleasant helpful manner which people appreciated. Half way through the proceedings, a serious young man gave a rousing political address and was roundly applauded by everyone including the offender. Then followed more witnesses giving evidence of disrespect to the court at the time in question until an elderly worker rose and said that in his opinion there was an element of vindictiveness in some of the accusations which the court ought to beware of. It was possible to exaggerate things. He wished to point out that the girl had previously to his knowledge shown herself to be a good revolutionary. He would prefer that she was given a serious warning not to let this sort of behaviour happen again. Such in fact was the final course decided upon by the court to general acclaim after which everyone disbanded still talking vivaciously at half an hour before midnight.

Since 1969, Law Study Commissions have been re-organising Cuba's legal system with the participation of all Cuban organisations in the framing of major new laws. The draft law against loafing and absenteeism under discussion at the time of my visit was debated by over seventy thousand workers, housewives, professional people, and members of the armed forces some of whose suggestions became part of the final law.

Above left: Antonio Maceo
Above right: José Martí
Below left: Camilo Cienfuegos
Below right: Che Guevara

Fidel Castro in the Sierra
Rebel army

Above left: Rebel headquarters in the Sierra

Above right: Attack on Moncada

Below left: The 26th of July School City now stands on the grounds of the previous Moncada Barracks. It was built in the early years after victory to wipe out bitter memories and carry out a promise to replace military forts by schools.

The 26th July celebrations

Above: Round the José Martí monument.

Below: In Revolution Square Havana

Left: Fidel Castro speaks

Street scene

Primary school children waiting for school. Most belong to the Cuban Pioneers and wear the Pioneer badge on a red beret and the blue and white Pioneer scarf.

Children's Circle or day-care centre
Primary school in Havana

The author looking over the border from Havana to Matanzas

Countryside school (Secundaria Básica)

Fishing school

Guamá, in the fenlands of Cuba's southern coast, showing the round, palm-thatched, Indian-type bohio where the author spent two nights in October 1971.

Sombreros!

Indian Zebu cows for heat resistance
crossed with Aberdeen and Holstein
pedigree bulls to give a stronger breed
and good milk yield

Veterinary students

Sugar

Mechanised cutting of sugar

A woman cane cutter

Sugar mill

Facing page

Left: Where lemons are part of the Citrus Fruit Plan

Right: Girl tractor drivers are a common sight in the orchards of modern Cuba as part of the work-study programme

Middle: Sampling chilli peppers

Below: Tobacco growing under awnings

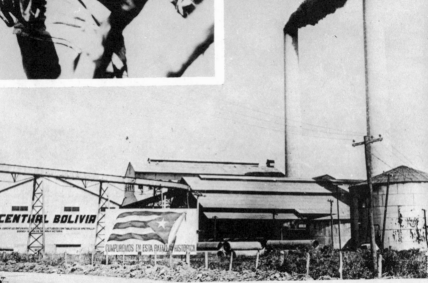

Old Trinidad

In the Historical Museum

A beautiful colonial house now the home of the Union of Writers and Artists of Cuba

Hemingway's old home is today a museum

The campaign against illiteracy

Right: Wall newspaper of a Committee for the Defence of the Revolution (the Malecon, Havana)

Left: Example of Cuba's new poster design

la habana 63   VII congreso de la
unión internacional
de arquitectos

Libertad
Libertad
Libertad
Libertad
Libertad

Angela
Angela
Angela
Angela
Angela
Angela

Sis
Lucho
Por
que
exista
La
Igualdad
en
Mi
Pays
Para
que
todos
tengamos Los mismos
los Vienes

Hugo Gonzalez, eleven years, greatly desired an Angela Davis badge that the author was wearing when they met in the street. He arranged a rendezvous by phoning her at her hotel, brought along his own interpreter (aged twelve) and offered this drawing he had made of the black American militant as a swap. Unfortunately the badge had been promised already but he gave the drawing as a keepsake.

Badge of the Federation of Cuban Women

Painting by a nine-year-old, Odalys Gatto, in the second grade
Seeing a film for the first time

REBEL YOUTH

IT WAS Che Guevara in *Socialism and Man in Cuba* who said: 'In our country the Party and Youth are important.' I was therefore particularly interested to have a leisurely talk with a representative of the Union of Young Communists (UCJ). Our meeting took place in the offices of *Rebel Youth* the young people's newspaper run by the Young Communists that was read in the early 'seventies by a hundred and eighty thousand Cubans of all ages in three daily editions (one for Havana and two for the rest of the island). Its headquarters, with the plate glass frontage, was used by the press before the revolution and was not unlike its counterpart in Fleet Street though transformed inside by the gay posters of the revolution.

My appointment was with a young man who was in his early teens when the Fidelistas marched triumphant into Havana. He answered my questions with that directness and expressive flow which one learns to expect from Cuba's young leaders.

Our discussion started with the paper of which he had once been assistant editor. I referred to its name 'Rebel Youth'. To be rebellious one has to have something to rebel against. What were the objects of rebellion in Cuba today? We agreed that, since a revolution was a continuing process, there were still many hangovers from the past to rebel against, bureaucracy to guard against and as long as there were oppression and hunger and imperialist wars anywhere in the world there were plenty of targets for rebellion.

Rebel Youth first appeared in 1962 as a weekly. It is now a daily and the only newspaper to appear on Sunday. Subject matter is wide, covering sports, cultural activities, production as well as the directly political field. It employs professional journalists in all regions many of whom are very young and have not finished their training. Besides professionals there are a large number of voluntary reporters in factories and farms. I asked were there debate and correspondence columns and was told the last Congress of Young Communists had decided to stimulate discussion in this and other ways.

Except for the children's newspaper *Pionero*, it is the only youth newspaper and demand is much greater than supply. Various youth magazines are published of which *Youth and Technology* has a circulation of forty thousand.

Talk next centred on the Union of Young Communists itself. What proportion of the membership I wondered were girls? And the answer was interesting. The national proportion was thirty per cent female but in the countryside girls formed a far lower proportion than this average figure.

'The reason,' he said, 'lies in our underdevelopment and the fact that historically women took little part in production or, for that matter, in society generally.'

More surprising, perhaps, was the fact that at the time out of fifty members of the national committee only three were girls. In the localities, however, apparently the proportion of young women in the leadership was growing progressively.

To become a member of the Union of Young Communists involves a highly selective process. 'Your name is put forward at a meeting of workmates or fellow students, or in the case of the military a unit of the Revolutionary Armed Forces. Each candidate is asked whether or not he wishes his nomination to be discussed. If he agrees the valuation is exhaustive. It includes consideration of attitudes to work and production, contribution to voluntary work, help given to others and relationships with workmates as well as contribution to the country's defence. All these factors are considered by a meeting of workmates. Finally the assembly votes and the nominations go forward to a committee at a higher level, after which another assembly of the whole collective is called to hear which names in the list of vanguard workers they submitted have been accepted.

I asked what happens if the assembly disagrees with the selection and was told that because of the degree of preliminary discussion this does not tend to happen but in any case a name not accepted could be proposed later.

I also asked about the generation of young people now growing up in revolutionary Cuba who in actual experience know nothing of the sufferings and struggles of the past. He replied that of course they were aware that there could be problems here and that others had met them. 'We try to give the young responsibilities which make them feel they are participants in the processes we are living through. Each generation has extremely difficult and challenging targets to fulfil in relation to its own time. We try to avoid making young people feel like spectators. At the same time we try to equip them for the cultural and technical revolution essential to us if we are to lift ourselves out of underdevelopment.'

So far we had been talking in terms of big numbers and, since sometimes it helps in understanding a big change over in society to examine what it means in terms of a life of an individual, I asked this young Cuban if he would mind telling me a little of his own history. His reaction told me something about the new kind of person Cuba is developing. He obviously was not enjoying this particular question and commented: 'Well, here we think in terms of working collectively rather than individually.' I explained my reasons for making so personal a request and he immediately without fuss responded.

The struggle against Batista under the command of Fidel Castro, he explained, united most sections of Cuban society.

'Like Fidel himself, I came from a petit bourgeois family and suffered no childhood deprivation. I went to a private school and was educated to anti-communism and at the time had all the normal aspirations of a lad of fourteen.' As an adolescent he sympathised with the aims of the 26th July Movement and when the Revolution came to power, he took part in student mobilisation in the town of Santa Clara, in the struggle against counter-revolution and those elements in the church who identified with it. 'Most important thing for

123

me,' he added, 'was that during this experience I saw that the Revolution carried out its promises and was just.'

During this time he studied at the University of Santa Clara and joined the militia. Then when the attack came at the Bay of Pigs, he was one of those mobilised to defeat it. 'It was in the course of these activities that I came to realise that I was a Marxist by belief,' he said.

His studies at the university were interrupted when he was asked to dedicate himself full time to youth and he was still waiting to go back and complete his studies after nine years. But during this time he had acquired rich experience, travelling in his work over the whole country, acting as sub-editor for the newspaper, gaining knowledge of industry and a great many other things.

I listened, moved by his frankness and modesty and thought as I was to do many times in the next few months. I hope these committed young leaders, whose wisdom and maturity Cuba needs so much, by living at such intensity do not burn themselves out.

SUNDAYS IN HAVANA

SINCE DAYLIGHT lorries have been speeding along the Malecon – the broad esplanade that runs the length of Havana's seafront – taking volunteer workers to help in the fields. The previous night we had seen on television the Cuban Prime Minister with President Allende on a visit to Chile. Unveiling a monument to Che Guevara, he told the Chileans how Che never kept a Sunday to himself, but every Sunday used to go out to some work centre, 'sometimes to the docks to load freight with the longshore-men, sometimes to the mines to work with the miners, sometimes to the fields to cut cane'. Che Guevara's style of volunteer work remained a prominent feature of the Cuban revolution during the 'sixties. In the 'seventies the emphasis may have changed but it is still seen as a cornerstone in the education of a revolutionary.

How I wondered, do Cuban families not engaged on voluntary work spend their weekend leisure? I knew that an increasing number were finding their ways to the beaches but I decided to have a look at Sunday in Havana.

By 8 a.m. the sun had already warmed the stones and Sunday fishermen were cutting up fish and casting out their lines as I took the sea road towards the ancient Morro Fort. Many early voyagers in their journals use the term beautiful to describe Havana and on this brilliant morning it was easy to see why. Juan Perez de Riva in 1697 saw Havana as a small city with low walls to the landward of about four thousand inhabitants living in houses of one storey. 'The women,' he wrote, 'are very beautiful and the men of agreeable appearance.' Two centuries later, the German poet George Werth saw Havana as large as Berlin, Brussels and

125

Lyons and partially resembling Paris . . . 'The more I know of Havana and the island of Cuba,' he wrote, 'the more I like them. Rio de Janeiro, Lima and Havana are the most beautiful cities I have seen in America, but Havana is the crown among them.' Havana struck both travellers as a city of great contrasts, the degradation of slavery and poverty side by side with rich and elegant living. Prophetically the German poet wrote: 'I believe that Havana may well be the place where the struggle for waging the great conflicts of the New World will be waged.'

A twentieth-century traveller writing in the *Geographical Magazine* of November 1959, at the time when this prophecy was coming true, described the Cuba that the revolution inherited as Spain translated into the tropics heavily influenced by the American way of life.

'American influence in Cuba,' he wrote, 'is particularly marked in Havana which is one of the most beautiful and cosmopolitan capitals in the western hemisphere. Its reputation for fast living seems largely dependent on neon lights, a couple of spectacular floor shows at the leading night clubs and a really astonishing number of touts offering to sell one anything and everything. Then of course there are the gambling casinos . . . Tourists, after sugar, provide the most important source of foreign exchange in Cuba. They pour into the country from the States and every day during the season (December-April) a stream of planes from Miami decant their cargoes of jungle-shirted and mink-stoled *vacationes* who take over the fashionable suburbs – that and the long, lovely beach resort of Veradero, some seventy miles from the capital. Few tourists venture further afield.'

What would these travellers have thought of Havana in the nineteen-seventies? Of the José Martí Park where on that Sunday young folk of all colours were playing and training together? Of the new fully-furnished apartment blocks facing the sea built by a crack team of building workers for other workers who in their turn were putting in plus-hours of work to meet Cuba's urgent need for more buses? Or for that matter, of the lines of weekend washing hung from the front balconies of faded colonial mansions showing that those who did the work were in possession now?

I found that when I expressed admiration at the architecturally imaginative and new in Havana, my Cuban hosts were careful to stress that many grave problems of overcrowding and poor housing remained to be solved and indeed the great backlog of repair work to be done is very evident. Hence the CDR posters declaring 'With the help of everyone we will beautify and clean up our city'. Housing needs have made the white helmets of the builders as popular a symbol of heroism as the machete of the cane cutters. These mini-brigades of high speed workers have been selected by their workmates from various industries to help tackle the housing shortage with a guarantee that their share in production will be made up during their absence from their own industry. Working with technicians, men with little or no previous experience have in three years transformed a wasteland eight miles from Havana into a small modern town, with its own sports and recreation centres, shops and nursery schools landscaped among hundreds of newly-planted shrubs and trees on the sea coast.

However, my destination that morning was not the new estate but Old Havana and the Cathedral Square. Boarding the 82 bus proved quite an experience in itself. At first there was room to breathe but we soon filled up to a good crush with small shrimps of boys wriggling their way through to strategic positions. In order to release labour for more productive jobs, no one collects fares on Havana buses. You drop a small coin in a box which takes you cheaply anywhere on the route. Apparently not everyone's socialist conscience comes up to standard and there is some doubt whether this obviously sensible arrangement can continue. However, I watched carefully and all including the children dropped in their coins on this occasion. Meanwhile we were hurtling through Havana to goodness knows where when my neighbour, a minute, fairhaired woman of late middle age, seeing my anxious gaze enquired where I was going and managed to convey that she too was going to the Cathedral and would show me the way. I looked upon this as a surprising piece of luck and accepted gratefully.

Cathedral Square

She led me to the small ancient square – one of the most complete examples in Havana of the enclosed medieval plaza. Very quiet it was this Sunday morning with the early morning sun throwing leaf patterns on the cobbled street. All the buildings surrounding the square are early eighteenth century. On three sides are the early palaces of the old nobility and their descendants. They are well preserved and are now used as craft centres and studios for a rich variety of Cuban crafts. Some of these ingeniously make use of local raw materials – the dried fruits and stems of plants, the waste from the sugar making process and, for sculpture, the precious hard woods of Cuba's forests.

Presiding over the square to the north is the yellowing stone edifice of the Cathedral with its open iron cross, its columns and its two towers containing the clock and the great bells. Built by a Jesuit order, the Cathedral started life as la Iglesia de San Ignacious in 1749 but its building was interrupted by the expulsion of the order and it was not consecrated as a cathedral until 1787.

As we entered, a central circular window threw slabs of red and blue light on the stone floor and a small choir was singing. My companions passed under the round arches of the aisles while I sat in a back pew glad of the rest. A group of boys playing in Cathedral Square looked in momentarily at the door and were gone without comment. Some forty people made up the congregation, among them a few young people with their parents. Presently a little girl distributed a hymn sheet and the congregation rose to sing. I listened for a while, then taking advantage of the pause before the address, returned once more to the dazzling sunlight of the world outside.

Two years later I was to return to the square and the

Cathedral on a spring night when lights in the houses showed up the beauty of their windows against dark walls and a courtyard fountain spread its spray over ferns bright green under the yellow lamplight. In the Cathedral, too, many crystal lights lit up the gentle domes of its ceiling and an organ was playing to a congregation of some two hundred people for a special occasion.

Although Santaria, the religion practised by former Yoruba slaves in Cuba, is today the strongest and most widespread religious grouping, the bulk of the population is still formally buried and baptised in the Roman Catholic Church. About twelve per cent are of the Roman Catholic or Protestant faith with the former greatly in the majority.

Since 1960-61 religious instruction has been confined to the churches. The nationalisation of private schools most of which were church schools, led to the exodus of many nuns. Many priests and methodist pastors also left the country after the Bay of Pigs invasion period. But even at that time of tension, in 1962, the revolutionary government rebuked 'hot headed extremist elements who want to declare war on religion, who sometimes do not respect the religious feelings of believers. The Revolution does not approve of these tendencies. The Revolution has taken serious measures to break up the Catholic hierarchy but it has done nothing to offend the sincere Catholic of the people. On the contrary it has guaranteed the rights of believers to their worship and their religion.'

Present day church-state relationships were summarised by the Cuban Prime Minister in an interview with a Mexican publication, *Sucsesos,* in 1966: 'No religious problem or atmosphere of tension exists between the Revolutionary Government and the Roman Catholic Church. Our relations are normal. Furthermore the Vatican has sent us an intelligent young man, Monsignor Zacchi, as its delegate to Cuba who has perfectly understood the social change that is developing our country. In Cuba no one is persecuted as long as they do not take part in counter-revolutionary activity. In the beginning the Catholic Church was used by the oligarchy to combat revolutionary changes. One must take into account that the Catholic religion has not been widespread among peasants, and relatively little among the poorer sections in general. On the other hand, the great bourgeoisie and the land-owners had been educated in Catholic schools. This produced some difficulties at the beginning.'

Relations today between church and state were likewise described by the Rector of the Roman Catholic San Carlos Seminary, Carlos Manuel de Céspides, in an interview first printed in *Cuba Internaciónal* (1970):

'We are not unaware of course of the divergence between the Marxist and Christian concepts of man and his world but neither are we unaware of the points of contact and the enormous possibilities of collaboration in the construction of the new Cuba. Conversely we also get the impression that Cuban Marxism seems to regard the church in a different light from 1961.'

Havana's museums

Across the square from the Cathedral, one of the ancient residences houses the Museo Colonial with its historic collection of furniture of the Spanish colonial period. Today a militia man is sitting outside combining guard duty with studying the news. Contrary to a press notice, the museum does not open until later but he lets me into the patio, very cool and beautiful with its dark leaved plants and white iron seats. All round the quadrangle runs an arcade that supports the galleries and a wide central staircase leads up to the furnished grande salle above. As in all houses of the prosperous classes in the colonial period, the living quarters are grouped round an open yard or patio, a device that keeps the houses fresh and cool. Typical too are the coloured glass fanlights which subdue the tropical glare of the sun as it filters into the interior.

At the height of the sugar trade in the eighteenth century, these palaces of the sugar barons gave a special tone to urban life. The ground floor was often converted into warehouse space for the merchants while they and their families lived on the top storey, the gallery linking their separate rooms. In between the two levels of the great house, a retinue of slaves, some twenty or thirty or even a hundred strong, spent their lives serving both the commercial and the domestic needs of their masters.

Today visitors to the museum can study the changing characteristics of Cuban design during Spanish colonial times: the sixteenth-century period when construction was based on the Indian bohio with wood as the main material; the seventeenth century characterised by a strong Spanish influence and simple organisation of space, with wood still the main material determining decorative expression; the development in the second half of the eighteenth century and early nineteenth when growth of international trade brought richer architecture and more elaborate furnishing with wrought iron appearing alongside wood in balustrades and doors; finally the neo-classical period of the second half of the nineteenth century which retained the patio as the nucleus of the house but replaced arcades with pillars and made great use of iron.

Revolutionary Cuba uses its museums to help Cubans of all generations to feel themselves heirs to their own history, and now many a small town has its local museum showing the region's share in the island's independence struggles. I remember the words of the curator of Havana's National Museum: 'You see we are re-constructing the museum while at the same time people are continuing to use it. We have been deprived of our cultural heritage too long to be able to mark time while buildings are being perfected.'

Vivid memories of the Museo de Belles Artes include seventeen-year-old medical student Angela whose spare time interests are painting, music and languages. I was already reeling from the impact of colour, decorative inventiveness and the breath-taking range and variety of Cuban painting when she replaced her friend the official guide as he had to leave for a class. Angela had the whole of Cuban painting at her finger tips and her passionate love for the work revealed much to me both about Cuban art and about Cuban young people. I jotted down the names of the artists to whose work I wished to return again and again: Porto Carrera and Marcelo Pogolotti, Serrando Cabrera Morena and Ángel Acosta León, Eduardo Abela, Wilfredo Lam, Victor Manuel Garcia, Amelea Pelaez and in the new Op Art and Pop Art section with its modern, witty and specifically Cuban version of social significance, the works of Raúl Martínez, Antonio Vidal and Fayad Jamis.

Not that the national agencies sit back and wait for people to come to the museums. Exhibitions are taken into the streets. During one week every shop window the length of a main street displayed examples of the folk art of Latin America. Similarly Cuba's new and adventurous poster art pinpoints the major social issues in striking colour on the street murals. Since there is no commercial advertising and private car traffic was almost non-existent, conditions lend themselves to street display.

The harbour side

In contrast to the quiet of Cathedral Square, the harbour a few streets away presented a lively scene with new Soviet and Cuban ships attracting the gaze of bystanders. Under the stern gaze of Cuba's oldest castle keep (the Castilla de la Fuerza built in 1588-1677 in the Plaza de Armas) families were fishing in the moat. I sat among them on the grass to watch. With large jars and a huge variety of improvised nets from shopping bags on the end of a string to little home made containers of perforated metal, the children, enthusiastically aided by their fathers, were catching a variety of small minnow-sized fish, blue streaked and yellow spotted. It was noticeable in these family parties that gentle and affectionate physical contact was a constant part of communication between the very young and their bigger brothers and sisters. I saw no child hit or shouted at in my stay in Cuba. The family nearest me – mum, dad, and two boys – had brought a large loaf of bread with them, partly for the fish and partly for themselves. It was they who told me that one of the most popular places to visit on Sunday was a fine new aquarium which I had already visited on the sea front where every fish that lives in Cuban waters can be seen in natural conditions in water constantly replenished from the sea.

Spick and span in carefully-laundered cotton clothes, boys and girls looked bright as new pins and twice as colourful. I was interested to see the unrationed coloured plastic sandals among the more solid and durable footwear. Running barefoot on tropical soil used to bring to the children of the poor the horrors of intestinal worm infestation which by blocking evacuation led to death when the worms would pour out from nose and mouth in search of another live host. This is perhaps one reason why in Cuba when there was shoe rationing one did not see barefoot children. The other reason is that though there were fewer shoes nobody got more shoes than they needed while others got none at all.

At night the harbour is studded with lights, those of the ships merging with lights in the houses of Casa Blanca seeming, too, to be floating on the far shore of the bay, while the harbour beacon flashes its warning light and the ferry boat adds its twinkling few to the general blaze.

I was told that a comprehensive plan for modernisation and reconstruction of the whole port area is already well under way, with technical and financial help from the Soviet Union. Many of the present port installations date back to the beginning of the century and now that Cuba's trade comes from far afield, the port is unfitted to cope with its scale and variety. The new plans include a terminal for containers and an unloading point for giant tankers as well as construction shops to repair and service port equipment. Havana's fishing port too, built largely on land recovered from the sea, is now one of the largest in Latin America. (The total annual fishing catch has increased six times since the revolution.)

133

Other finds on Sundays included a small theatre where children of the neighbourhood were watching puppet plays, a trade union social centre, a children's free cinema and a seaside recreation centre where, besides the usual helter-skelters, there was a miniature Indian village to play in. Here too a joint birthday party was in full swing. The birthday cake, packet of candies for each child, Disney-type party decorations, excited children and weary grown-ups were all reminiscent of similar events at home when wartime rationing made such events an extra special treat. Later that evening teenage sisters and brothers were among the large audience of a pop drama festival put on by units of the Revolutionary Armed Forces with singers, actors and musicians drawn from their own ranks. Others lucky enough to procure a ticket from their trade union were waiting for entrance to the cabaret at the famous Tropicano show, now running with a difference, under the auspices of the Tourist Commission (INIT). Still others, like myself were streaming into the City Sports Auditorium to see Cuba's star gymnast, Sonia Pedrosa, in the international tournament of modern rhythmic gymnastics, very beautiful to watch and popular in Cuba. But on hot spring and summer nights, the whole of old Havana seems to be out of doors either strolling in the streets and filling the broad tree-lined length of the Prado, or on the Malecon sitting on the sea wall with their background the ocean and in front the myriad lights of the city stretching up to the stars.

CHILDREN'S LITERATURE IN CUBA

THE FACTS and figures of leisure time reading of Cuban children I had received from the children's section of the excellent José Martí National Library but it was on the broad surface of the sea wall that I encountered for the first time a publication that goes into most homes where there are young children. Someone's fishing line had hooked a barracuda, fierce fish of tropical waters with a fiendish bite, and a group of small boys had gathered to watch its skilled handling by an old fisherman. In the general excitement a magazine had been left behind on the wall which caught my eye because it had all the appearance of one of our own children's comics. Printed boldly in gradations of tangerine and black, it turned out to be *Pionero,* the children's weekly published by the Union of Pioneers (the nearest equivalent to our Scouts and Guides and Woodcraft Folk). On the cover was a cartoon of a little girl with short pigtails, tied in bows Cuban-fashion, and dressed in the white blouse and pleated skirt of Cuban school uniform. Against a design of pedestrian crossing symbols she was blowing out her cheeks on a large whistle while holding up her hands to the oncoming traffic. It was, in fact, Road Safety Campaign week in Havana and her counterpart in real life was conducting traffic at school crossings at other points in the city.

It was a curious sensation to find at least three pages of *Pionero* were devoted to a weekly serial of children's classics by British writers. One was a cartoon version of *Peter Pan* and the other Robert Louis Stevenson's *Treasure Island* believed to be based on the magically beautiful, once bandit-haunted, Isle of Pines off the south-west coast of Cuba, now renamed the Isle of Youth after all the young people who have helped in its development. The centre of the magazine was reserved for illustrated excerpts from a famous Cuban child's classic, one of the few in the history of Cuba to be written especially for children. This was *The Golden Age* by José Martí.

During my stay in Cuba, two special numbers of *Pionero* appeared. One was a baseball special to mark the world baseball championship in Havana. This carried details of the main players, a free gift of a baseball stamp album and the history of a famous guerrilla who was also an ace baseball player. The other special edition commemorated Che's life and death. For this a journalist Anisia Miranda paid a visit to a school and asked the children what impressed them most about Che's life? What did Che think about imperialism? (Answer: That they want to govern everyone and must be stopped. They are lazy and do not want to work but want others to work for them.) What did they feel when they heard he had died? (Answer: I felt as though my father had died. People cried in Revolution Square – I saw them.) What example did they think he left everyone? (Answer: That we must help all people and all children to be free. That people must not be selfish. That they must be disciplined in combat. Fidel asked us all to learn to be like Che.) This interview filled the centre pages together with a photo-montage of children's faces and scenes from the life of their hero. Elsewhere there as usual was Peter Pan with the pirates and Long John Silver, a page about the trees of Cuba, pictures to colour and a cartoon about adventures with 'zernies' from outer space.

By a happy coincidence I was visiting Cuba at a time when the whole question of children's literature was very much in the air. A few months previously, it was a main subject of discussion at the First National Congress of Education and Culture when speakers pointed to the crying need for literature, films and television specially written and devised for children, and Fidel Castro pointed out in reply that not only Cuba but most of the world lacked these things. He thought the solution lay, not in continually looking to a comparatively small group who in the past had monopolised the name of intellectuals but in encouraging a wide artistic and literary movement among the people. He was sure, for instance, that Cuba's hundred thousand teachers had enough talent and imagination between them to supply these needs and give Cuba her own children's literature.

It should, of course, be understood that as regards educational publishing there has been a phenomenal development in the last fifteen years. The Cuban Book Institute, created in 1967, raised publishing levels to twenty eight million units in 1972-73, mostly educational books distributed free to students. In pre-revolutionary Cuba there was almost total deprivation for the country child and for many town children as far as books were concerned. Educational books have priority over all forms of publishing but thousands of *becadoes* – pupils of the new boarding schools – are already stretching out hands for far more books than the Book Institute can supply.

It was to discuss some of these questions that I met three Cuban poets at the Cuban Writers Union one intensely hot afternoon. We sat and talked in the comparative cool of a garden of what was once the home of a wealthy banker and now serves as the headquarters of UNEAC (Union of Writers and Artists of Cuba). Conversation was direct thanks to the fluent English of Professor Eliseo Diego, one of Cuba's well-known poets, a Catholic Marxist whose poetry was first published in 1920. He was at the time in charge of the juvenile section of the José Martí National Library which was currently holding an exhibition of children's writings and paintings. With him were two members of the editorial board of *La Gaceta de Cuba* the Union's monthly gazette: the poet Luis Marré, for many years a member of the Cuban Communist Party, whose work has been much translated abroad and Adolfe Suárez, one of the many young poets and writers of the post-revolutionary period.

I asked them how they felt about writing for children? Were there special historical reasons apart from the more obvious ones for the slow development of a specifically Cuban children's literature? Eliseo Diego reminded me that in the small island of Cuba was written the most important of all works for children in Latin America – *The Golden Age* by José Martí (which I had just read in *Pionero*). But, he added, it took a truly great man like José Martí to break through the traditional attitude in Spanish culture that considers writing for children an unmanly occupation. Today, he said, even with the revolution in full swing, there still remains to be conquered a hangover from the past and a persistent obstacle – the disdain with which the male in Latin American cultures regards all things to do with the care of children, looking upon these as the concern only of nursemaids or grandmothers – and included in this category was writing poems, stories and plays for children.

Professor Diego differentiated between genres of children's books – those on which children exercise their sensibilities and those from which they primarily acquire knowledge. He admitted that some writers have the delicate touch which enable them to combine both genres but he considered that this was a very difficult task. The best children's books of the first type, he thought were more akin to the world of poetry where child and adult were one.

On the present day development of children's literature he said: 'We need it as badly as we need bread itself. It was once the fashion to think that art in education was a mere adornment like icing on the cake. But on the contrary, through the special medium of language I believe literature exercises a decisive influence on the sensibility and the imagination and without imagination and sensibility what we call the new man would run the risk of not being a man at all . . . I am everlastingly stressing the supreme importance of the aesthetic factor in these matters. a really good tale for children begins and ends with being a good tale. If it is really a good tale it performs a role as important as history or arithmetic. In my opinion there is no need to artificially implant a moral. Aesthetics are as important as ethics.'

I was interested to see these opinions in print in the current issue of *La Gaceta de Cuba* which contained a selection of imaginative writing for children by foremost Cuban writers: *The Fables of Cuba* recreated by Miguel Barnet, a play for a puppet theatre by Dora Alonso, *Songs for Children* by David Cherican. The editorial took the form of an interview with Eliseo Diego in which he was asked what advice he would give to someone who wished to write books for children. He replied: 'Do it for the pleasure of doing it and knowing that you fulfil a great need. The best books for children have never arisen merely from good intentions but have come from the same source of inspiration as the Divine Comedy and the Iliad. You need to read a great deal and have the whole of language at your fingertips. Children constitute the most exacting of publics. I do not want to discourage anyone: only to point out that writing for children is a most difficult task and one, moreover, that is worthy of being tackled by the best of us. Here in our country all opportunities are there. The writer for children in Cuba needs no more than the desire to write and the consciousness that in making a book that children can call their own, he is fulfilling a duty in which José Martí set us the first example.'

A small incident immediately following this discussion with the Cuban poets remains in my memory. I left UNEAC with a selection of attractively designed books which gave some idea of the prolific amount of poetry and prose being produced in revolutionary Cuba. These were lying on the seat of the car when, owing to a slight mishap, we ran into a traffic pile-up. Children were coming out of school and, as would happen in the same circumstances in any city in the world, the accident drew them like a magnet and soon a little group had their noses under the bonnet along with the driver and the militia men. One small boy looked into the car and was politely interested until he saw the colourful collection of books on the seat. Then I was forgotten and the engine was forgotten. He was obviously itching to get his hands on the books and positively shone with pleasure when requested to transfer them to the relief car that came to take us home. I thought of him months later when I heard that the Union of Pioneers of Cuba and the National Council of

Culture were running a nation-wide competition for the best poetry, stories, plays and songs for children, and hoped that it would provide something for him and all the other children whose lively company I enjoyed in Cuba.

A conversation resumed

When two and a half years later I was able to resume my conversation with Professor Eliseo Diego, I was able to ask how far this hope had been fulfilled.

'Things have improved a lot in relation to the number of titles for children by Cuban authors since you were here last,' he told me. 'There is still some way to go yet as regards quality because our new writers are mostly very young and,' he added with a twinkle, 'like young people everywhere they think they know best but there is great interest and some significant new developments.

'It has, for instance, long been my obsession that the Union of Writers annual literary contests should include a prize at the same level for children's literature in order to break through the mental barrier caused by the old myth that writing for children was unfit for grown men.' (He quoted Walter de la Mare: 'The best is not good enough for children.') 'Now such an award has been instituted and attracted many entrants. Casa de las Americas, too, has for the first time in history included children's books in its book competitions and with over a hundred writers responding from all over Latin America, the result should be significant for a continent where, as in Cuba, the need is for books based on a country's own culture. Again, the Armed Forces of Cuba, perhaps the only army in the world that initiates cultural activity covering all art and literature, now by a similar award stimulates the writing of books for children by its members.

'Apart from a growing number of children's books by new Cuban writers some of our best known authors have begun to write in this field. For example the distinguished poet

Mirta Aguirre has just published a delightful book of her poems for children that would rank with the best in any language.'

Professor Diego also referred to recent developments relating to literary agreements with Socialist countries by which Cuban books were printed in the German Democratic Republic and elsewhere and books from the socialist countries were published in Cuba. He considered one of the best joint ventures was an anthology of Russian poems for children, sensitively translated by the combined efforts of Cuban and Soviet translators.

Following a national discussion meeting in 1972 on young people and children's literature, a permanent advisory commission was appointed from outstanding Cuban intellectuals to coordinate work in this field in conjunction with the Young People's Publishing House *Nueve Gente*. In a room in what was previously a private residence where this editorial house of the Book Institute carries out its activities, we met its director Sonia and her assistant Margaly, two young women in their twenties or thirties whose infectious enthusiasm left one confident of the future of this venture. They told us their aim was to help children explore their world through books from a very early age by means of familiar things and in terms of their own stage of development in such a way that they grow up to feel no realm of knowledge is closed to them or reserved for the specially gifted. They have plans, too, with the help of child psychologists to keep close contact with their readers to whom the publishing house belongs, recording their suggestions and reactions to books published. We were told also of a plan to hold a children's book festival during the summer holidays. On the first day writers and illustrators from other countries as well as Cuban writers would be invited so that children could meet them and discuss. Then would be the time for them to besiege and surround the writers with their demands and suggestions. Books to handle, puppets, plays, story-telling and live examples of Cuba's birds and beasts – all this would be there against the seaside setting of the

Pioneer's National Camp at Veradero. I accepted an invitation to attend on the spot!

In the Children's Department of the National Library of Cuba a striking feature was the combination of painting, reading and the children's own writing. Walls were covered with children's illustrations to books read and I was shown a book of stories for children by children, illustrated by themselves and containing a selection from many more that were written for a national contest. Literary circles meet weekly and there is also a room for story telling, dimly lit and strewn with cushions where children sit listening to tales told in the oral folk traditions of Cuba. About two hundred children, I was told, pass through this library in a week. Other parts of Cuba too have their bookshops and little reading rooms combined as I discovered when I visited Santiago de Cuba as a guest of the new Oriente Publishing House. Here a mural was the collective effort of small children from the mountainous districts of the Sierra Maestra and the shop window was full of children's paintings of books they had read.

A year and a half ago enough reading books were published for each Cuban child to have only one each. In 1974 enough were published to provide each child with two or three. So although Cuban literature for children is still in its infancy, since my last visit the scene has changed appreciably.

Finally curiosity to see how *Pionero* was progressing led to a meeting with its editorial board from whom I learnt that every class and every school has its *Pionero* representative. Still catering for ages nine to twelve, there were changes in content but not in appearance. The comic strip style, popular with its readers, seemed even more prominent. (The Walt Disney touch is visible in many illustrations to children's books.) There was a cartoon series based on the history of Cuban independence struggles, a similar one related to Latin America, and another based on a Soviet secret service tale of the Second World War. Besides puzzles and general knowledge quizzes, articles appear about the life of José Martí which are used in José Martí youth seminars, and there are also short stories about the lives of well-known figures in the history of the international communist movement. Important new features are a correspondence column with letters from readers and a readers' news column, in this case carrying news of the 'Clics' – pioneers who take on the job of reminding grown-ups and children to save electricity by clicking off unnecessary lights.

THE ARTS IN A CHANGING SOCIETY

CUBA'S NATIONAL Council of Culture co-ordinates a leisure time programme of inexpensive theatre, music and dance both professional and amateur. Some of the most popular performances in my experience were those presented by the Conjunto Folklorico Nacional, so popular that long before the theatre doors opened crowds thronged the streets outside. Before the 1959 revolution there was no institution whose specific task it was to keep alive the folk music and dance of Cuba but much interest had been stimulated by the work of the anthropologist Don Fernando Ortiz and already in the 'thirties genuine folklore groups flourished. Soon after the revolution, in 1960, there was created a department of folklore of the National Theatre of Cuba and two years later the National Folklore Conjunto came into being. Its members were described as men and women of the people, workers, students, artisans following their own trades, who together contributed a rich experience of the various traditions of African dance and song. 'It reveals the genius of a people for whom rhythm is innate. Its theme is the vitality of humanity and it is full of self confidence and optimism,' wrote a critic of *Paris Soir* after a tour of its dance company in France. Song and dance groups travel throughout Cuba playing to schools and cane harvesting camps, to factories and the armed forces. At the same time, various study circles attached to the Conjunto trace the roots of Cuba's folk music which has given the world beside the cha cha and the mambo, the work songs and revolutionary music of present day Cuba.

A Cuban language in cinema

Cinema has become one of Cuba's most important art

forms with an international reputation. INCAIC, the Institute of the Art and Industry of Cinema, was set up three months after victory in 1959. One of its directors outlined its aims to me.

'Before the Revolutionary Government nationalised the cinema a specifically Cuban cinema did not exist. Our aim was to create an authentic non-commercial cinema rooted in the traditions of our own culture, which could help to deepen understanding of ourselves and the changes taking place in society as part of the revolutionary education of our people. At the same time we wanted to change the quality of the audience, from a passive to a more active one, sufficiently informed to be able to assimilate critically. We wanted a public that was as it were on its guard. approaching cinema not as a magic myth but as a stimulus to intelligence. To do this we needed films that were different, more of a challenge and touching on problems in society both here in Cuba and in the world. None of this has been easy and we have a long, long way to go. Audiences have advanced but progress depends on raising our general cultural level. But the most important thing is that a Cuban language in cinema has been created that reflects our reality in our own way.'

I asked about the cinema and the countryside. 'We try to show the same quality of films in rural Cuba as in the cities, even if this means mobile film units travelling by donkey to the mountains or on boats to small islets off the coast. Each truck travels with a driver, a projectionist and a sociologist because we like to record audience reaction. Cuban audiences, as well as showing pleasure readily, also register irritation and even anger at something they do not like or are puzzled by and this makes such work very interesting. We have filmed the reactions of country children seeing films for the first time (Plate XX). Another experiment was to show films to five and seven-year-olds then give them paint and paper and ask them to make a poster for the film. The painting of these young children is sometimes very exciting and some of these posters we have printed and used nationally.'

One recent film delightfully reflects the reactions of school children to their new life in the countryside weekly boarding schools. Others seek to heighten awareness and understanding of problems that arise when people are adapting to changes in society. For instance a film that recently has won an international award *Usteden tienen la palabra* (It's up to you now) deals with a rural community whose whole life is being changed by new patterns of farming. In the individual conflicts of the village people audiences recognise their own frustrations. Bewilderment in a world of unfamiliar techniques, the grip of old prejudices holding back women, the feeling of being planned out of existence – contemporary experiences like these are aired on the screen so that burdens that seemed private, unique and insurmountable are seen as shared and often capable of solution. This particular film relies more heavily on verbal argument than most Cuban documentaries but it is an interesting example of cinema as group therapy as well as art and education.

So-called social realism in art and literature was a subject of a discussion I had with poet and Marxist Luis Marré who gave the opinion that social realism in its narrow sense was not part of the rich and diverse Cuban tradition though in its widest sense it could be applied to all art, including some very great art, that reflects the full dynamic life of people. He thought that the culture of a country thrives best on its own roots and the imposition of a foreign art tradition rarely produces great art.

It was Cuban film critic Enrique Colina who spoke of the need to avoid oversimplifying reality, when he wrote that a committed cinema must never make the process of revolutionary change seem less complex than it really is. It is this concern with the complexity of human life and social development that to date gives Cuban cinema its special vitality.

Ballet for everybody

Sunlight filtered through the coloured glass of the beautiful house in Havana which is the present home of the Ballet Academy of Cuba and here one late October afternoon I experienced at first hand the contagious enthusiasm of its director.

Mr Alonso speaks soft, fluent English. He explained that right from its beginning in 1948 the Ballet of Cuba followed a broad artistic line based on respect for the romantic and classical tradition, but drawing strength also from contemporary choreographers with national works forming a basic part of the repertoire.

Over the years, too, it has carried out what the company considers one of its most important tasks: the education of the whole people in a love for the ballet, taking it into the public squares, while always making the greatest effort to present work of the top quality, both out of respect to the audiences and from the belief that this was the best way to reach an audience naturally responsive to art.

I was particularly interested in the broad contact of the ballet school with the everyday life of Cuban children. In present day Cuba, dancers from the academy go out to nursery schools and play groups.

'We are starting with the toddlers,' said Fernando Alonso, 'and we are beginning quite simply with our feet right on the ground. No special buildings because these are not the essential thing – and the children's songs provide the music.

'It is important from the health angle because, probably connected with long years of unbalanced diet, quite a number of Cubans have poor posture and the proportion of flat feet is high. Of course we also keep our eyes open to find our dancers really young, because the sooner in life you start, the longer in life you can continue to dance. So there is this angle too.'

He explained that from the early days of the academy it had to overcome strong opposition to the idea of boys taking up ballet.

'But dance,' said Fernando Alonso, 'is a necessary outlet for the emotions for men as well as women. Both feel internal pressures at work and at home. Life is always difficult anyway.

'Art is a way of letting off steam – and dance as a form of artistic expression is particularly useful as a physical outlet. For children and young people art and play, as well as work, are essential for growth.

'Then of course,' he added, 'here in Cuba's revolution we are trying to find a correct basis for human behaviour – trying to change ourselves as we change society; trying to be more honest, less selfish and to care about our neighbours and the world. Art as the highest expression of man should help in this.'

By the time our talk ended it was twilight and the hour for an electricity cut in this section of Havana. But the walk round the house was curiously lovely in the half-light. A wide staircase led up to a large dance room with great beauty of proportion. In the centre of the building was the typical tiled quadrangle with coloured floor and the cool greenery of climbing plants. On one of its supporting pillars was a list of guard duty times for each ballet dancer – a reminder that this was a ballet school of revolutionary Cuba, a ballet school with a difference.

The school was created by the Alonsos in 1950 to train dancers for the company and was then known as the Alicia Alonso Ballet Academy. At first there was a small state subsidy but in the stormy years of the middle 'fifties this subsidy was withdrawn. Following the coup of Fulgencio Batista, the ballet refused an offer from him of official recognition, believing that acceptance would be tantamount to condoning the tyranny, and this was his reprisal.

Ballet was already one of the most loved forms of art in Cuba and anger at the withdrawal of the subsidy was widespread with workers and cultural organisations demonstrating in the streets. After a protest tour throughout the island, the company stopped giving performances and Alicia Alonso declared she would not dance in Cuba as long as Batista's regime remained in power. One of the first acts of the revolutionary government in 1959 was to pass a law fully

148

guaranteeing state protection to the company which became the National Ballet of Cuba.

World acclaim for the Cuban school of ballet and its prima ballerina Alicia Alonso has since been expressed in many international awards. After the 1959 revolution, as well as new productions of traditional ballets, many new ballets by Cuban and foreign choreographers have been staged, those with revolutionary content including the Cuban ballet *Woman*, a ballet based on Cuba's liberation entitled *Despertar* (*Awakening*) with music by the Cuban composer Carlos Farinas, *Vietnam – the lesson* by Alberto Alonso and *Conjugación* also by Alberto Alonso and inspired by the life and death of Che Guevara.

Cuban ballet is an example of the way revolutionary Cuba draws on past art forms that were originally created for the exclusive benefit of a leisured few and uses them to enrich the lives of everybody. It has lived through times of profound change and it was the British critic, Arnold Haskell, who has known three generations of Cuban dancers who said in a message to the company on the occasion of its twenty-fifth anniversary. 'The tradition remains not only intact but enhanced. I find your choreography of the greatest interest, truly creative and modern.'

'You may graft the world cultural heritage to the tree of our republics, but let the trunk continue to be that of our republics.' José Martí

Far ranging questions concerning the role of the arts in a changing society were debated at the First Congress of Education and Culture the year of my first visit to Cuba. Nearly eight thousand recommendations from prior discussions were received by delegates from Cuba's educational, cultural and political organisations. The congress emphasised Cuba's view of the importance of art in society and the influence it exerts on people's way of life and among its many conclusions it expressed the opinion that 'culture like education is not and cannot be non-political or impartial in

149

as far as it is a social phenomenon which throughout history has been conditioned by the needs of social classes and their struggles'. The overriding needs of Cuba's present stage of development as a socialist state were seen to require the development of Cuba's own forms and values 'which colonialism sought to destroy' and a big extension of the amateur movement in the arts in order to tap latent talents in the people, while at the same time opening doors wider on the arts of Latin America and 'absorbing all that is best in world culture without it being imposed from without'.

PART III
The Developing Countryside

FAREWELL HAVANA

JOURNALISTS AT their seventh International Congress held in Havana in 1971 will remember the words of Dr Carlos Rafael Rodriguez, member of the revolutionary government:

'Many of you will leave tomorrow without having had the chance to see anything outside the capital. I am quite sure your impression of Havana has been of a slightly discoloured city, with buildings lacking paint, the sadness of electricity cuts and the queue of shoppers. Perhaps some of you knew the other Havana painted bright and gay. That city was, as Fidel said, a facade for our hidden poverty. Gay Havana by night meant nothing but shame and infamy for our young women forced into prostitution by dire need. We are fully aware that one day we shall have to bring back light and colour to Havana but today our capital is a stagnant capital of a developing country.'

Desire to see this developing countryside was very strong when at last I met Carlos from the foreign press department but shortage of cars forbade hope. I was therefore overjoyed to learn that all was arranged for me to take a journey with him the length of the island to Oriente starting on the morrow. This left just time enough for a farewell look at Havana. It was the hour when hundreds of youngsters, all shades and all sizes, were strolling out of school with folders and books under their arms and this was Havana as I wanted to remember it. Later I counted nearly a hundred people waiting for the 6.15 bus to take them out to the suburbs but on the balconies of city houses groups of workers were already settling down for night classes. Nearer the sea young Cuba in sports rig-out was flooding into José Martí park where wrestling and baseball were in progress. Not far away the imaginative design of the Casa de Las Americas soared into the sky. Throughout the isolation imposed by the blockade, this centre has fostered links between various aspects of Latin American culture and currently running was a display of the rich tapestries of Violetta Parra into which Chile's famous singer and artist had woven the folk tales of her people. Havana on this last evening, discoloured buildings and electricity cuts and all, was a city I had grown to love and to which I wanted to return.

In Matanzas Province

Early next morning we departed. The route at first ran parallel to the coast where royal palms tower against the sky and the sea air is sweet with the scent of Cuba's national flower – the *mariposa* or butterfly tree. All along the route the old stands side by side with the new: the many remaining *bohios*, wooden shacks with palm-thatched roofs, beside the new farm cottages, rural schools and modern clinics while here and there oil drills are a feature of the changing landscape breaking into the flowing lines of orchards, sisal fields and sugar cane. Leaving Havana Province behind us, we entered the neighbouring province of Matanzas. The name means slaughter and some say recalls a massacre of native Indians. Three hundred years and more have passed since the first slave ship arrived bringing a new African slave labour force to Matanzas but there are still people in the province who were born into slavery and remember when these wooded hills overlooking the green Yumuri valley were the haunt of runaway slaves taking refuge in the Pan de Matanzas mountains. The songs of their people tell too about the bloody slave uprisings of the 1840s when a rebellion started by a slave gang in the Alcancia sugar mill spread to mill after mill and beyond to coffee plantation, cattle ranch and railroad throughout the province. After its suppression by the Spanish military, great numbers committed suicide rather than return to unendurable tyranny, leaving their aspirations and sorrow behind them in the songs of the province.

Today, through storm and calm a coral reef makes for still waters in the great bay of Matanzas city which throughout the centuries has been an important shipping point for sugar and tobacco. Here at its northern edge is Veradero, enchanting in its quiet beauty. It was once owned in its entirety by a foreign speculator who installed a private police force, private roads, hotels, chalets and gaming parlours. Today it is being developed as a worker's holiday centre. We arrived at Veradero for the night in time to see the white sands gleaming mile upon mile between the dark pines and the incredibly warm, translucent sea. The only people on the beach except myself that mild October were two girls who poured into my hands minute shells the colour of sunset – pink and yellow and mother-of-pearl. We walked together on the ribbed sand at the sea's edge, our splashing feet disturbing brilliant small creatures in the shallow waters. (Plate VI).

That evening after a meal in the plush surroundings of a former night club we retired early for a quiet talk. Tomorrow the plan was to continue the journey to the flat swamplands of the island's southern coast and see something of Cuba's new farming projects, so I used the opportunity to fill in gaps in my general knowledge of Cuban agriculture.

In few places in the world are there richer soils than those found in the valleys of Cuba and on a large proportion of their land throughout the island sugar cane is grown, a crop that thrives here perhaps better than anywhere else in the world. Tobacco growing is concentrated in three main areas: the plains to the south of the western mountains of Pinar del Río; an area to the south of Havana where much of the best leaf is grown, and in central Las Villas to the north of the Escambray mountains where the filler tobacco is produced. The home of cattle and dairy farming is on the plains of Las Villas and Camagüey where natural pastures cover poorer soil while further east on the mountains of Oriente a large part of Cuba's coffee is grown.

In pre-revolutionary Cuba the majority of country workers were not peasants living off the land they owned and rented.

They were wage earners used to working together on the *latisfundias*, big estates surrounding the sugar mills and ranches mostly owned by Cuban and foreign companies. (The Agricultural Census for 1946 recorded 423,690 farm labourers on 37,713 farms with an average employment of 4.1 months in the year). The revolutionary government therefore took the decision not to break up all these large estates into small parcels of land unsuited to mechanised agriculture which they considered would have been a backward step needing revision later. To quote Che Guevara: ·The Revolution made an agrarian reform for the first time in Latin America attacking property relations that were not feudal. There were a few feudal sections in tobacco and coffee which were given to small producers but sugar, rice and cattle lands were worked collectively in 1960.' Castro recently explained to the Small Farmers Association that the new concept of agrarian reform 'made it possible to keep workers as workers and this increased the power of the working class'.

Small farmers and their Association, however, have played an important part in the Cuban revolution and this remains true to the present day when they farm about thirty per cent of the land. Lowry Nelson in *Rural Cuba*, writing of the year 1945-6, said that small farmers although numerous had a pitifully small share of the land. While nearly three quarters of the farmers operated small tracts of land, their total area comprised only eleven per cent of all land in farms.

After 1959 the government agency responsible for agriculture, the National Institute of Agrarian Reform (INRA) was at first mainly staffed by Rebel Army men under the leadership of Captain Munez Jimenez but the president of INRA has been for many years Fidel Castro who made agriculture his abiding interest.

A citrus fruit plan

Cuba's state farming enterprises are often very big units

156

indeed. In southern Mantazas for instance groves of orange and lemon trees stretch like a vast green sea where less than ten years ago was rocky virgin soil. Thirty-three thousand acres of land now form part of the Victory of Girón Fruit Plan which hopes to be in full production at the end of the century and cover over two hundred thousand acres. Tests revealed suitable soils and an ample supply of underground water for irrigation, essential for fruit in the dry season. We could see from the soil map that young trees had been planted on the best red earth while elsewhere land was reserved for pineapples, coffee and, around the perimeter, sugar cane and root vegetables. Within the socialist countries Cuba is the only grower of citrus fruit, the secretary explained as we walked between the rows of seven-year-old orange trees with their great thick-skinned fruit glowing in the dense foliage. One priority task had been the training of agronomists specialising in fruit production of which there were extremely few in 1959. In the mid-seventies there were more than three hundred specialists of all kinds working in the area as well as trainee technicians gaining experience while studying.

For me the most interesting part of the plan was its tie-up with the countryside schools of the kind I had visited. Without the help of the schools, the fruit plan could not work and without their pupils' contribution to production Cuba could not afford the schools. Citrus fruit growing lends itself well to this sort of co-operation and a total of one hundred and twenty-four schools to house fifty-five thousand secondary school students are in the plan for the Victory of Girón fruit project.

At the time of my visit the state owned about five-eighths of the land covered by the scheme. The rest was worked by private owners who had previously farmed the area. I knew that in theory the Cuban leaders had set their face against any kind of coercion to force peasants to farm collectively. Government policy was to entice rather than coerce farmers to cooperate. Talking to the Small Farmers' Association in the early 'seventies Fidel Castro pointed out the advantages:

'All the little bits of land are joined together and not left idle. The workers in one plot join with the workers in another which results in infinitely better living conditions.' But he emphasised. 'The principle of waiting for land to be turned over voluntarily . . . must be respected absolutely. This has always been stated clearly and every time this principle is violated, it will cause a mess, because it will be a violation of our political and revolutionary principles.'

I asked a farmer member of the management committee how this worked out in practice. He said. 'If a farmer decides to hand over his land he is paid a good pension for life for the use of his land. This does not of course prevent him from continuing to work the land and draw a wage as a member of the collective. He is also rehoused in a new furnished apartment. Many peasants locally became very interested in the Victory of Girón scheme and some even gave their land to the revolution. Farmers who continue to own their land are required to farm it in keeping with the general plan. There is no coercion but there are strong social pressures towards joining the collective and living in the far better conditions of the new villages with their better all-round facilities.'

A fishing school

Cuba's revolutionary past, both recent and distant, is imprinted on the minds of children in a variety of ways. Foremost among them is the celebration of a long list of heroes and heroic events, both national and international, with whom Cubans identify their own struggles and hopes. On the tenth anniversary of the Bay of Pigs invasion, pupils from all over the island who had excelled in exams were given a holiday to follow the trail of historic landmarks that led to victory over the invading forces at Playa Girón on the southern shores of Matanzas Province. It was roughly this route that we travelled – from the sugar mill *Australia* which acted as headquarters for Fidel Castro and the command of

158

the Revolutionary Armed Forces, past the immense mangrove country of the Zapata Swamp, past the spot where now stands the little primary school named after General Antonio Maceo, the black general of the wars of independence, ending, since weather conditions made it impossible to see either of the historic beaches, in the fabulous national park where crocodiles kept for breeding lay dozing and grinning in the sun.

The south coast of the Zapata Peninsular is also the site of one of the revolution's schools for fisherboys known as the Victory of Girón School of Fishing and built in 1965. Here boys ranging in age between fourteen and seventeen most of whom have completed six grades of primary education, have for their use a training flotilla of five motor fishing boats, three sailing boats and several other small craft fitted with modern electronic equipment for navigation and fish finding. There is a hospital with its own laboratory, a laundry and a tailor's shop, a barbers, a bakery, a meteorological station and a theatre as well as practical rooms with modern navigational equipment. At the end of the course, which includes general education to eighth grade, the young fishermen qualify to join one of Cuba's three fishing fleets or if they wish they can transfer to an advanced fishing school in Havana. The course includes military training and discipline throughout is semi-military. This is seen as a necessary preparation for an occupation which dangerous in the normal run of events is doubly so for Cuban fishermen in the current situation where their fishing vessels have been liable to piratical attacks at sea (Plate XII).

History of a marsh

For two days we rested at Boca de Guamá which is reached by ferry across a fresh water lagoon to the east of the Bay of Pigs. Carlos explained that the place was originally conceived as a way of bringing tourist industry to the people of the marshes but isolation following the United States embargo and the decision of the Organisation of American States to boycott Cuba, put an end to this idea since when it has been mainly used for internal tourism and foreign guests. However with Cuba's growing links with her close neighbours in Latin America and the English-speaking states of the Caribbean the picture may well be about to change. Those who designed Guama based their ideas on native Indian forms where applicable, making maximum use of local materials and local craftsmen. Palm is used in every aspect, woven fronds for roofs and planks of palm for floors and walls and hand-made furnishings. Bohio-like cabins are reached by interlinking bridges crossing the lagoon, lit at night to create a fantasy world. In one of these I spent the night alone with the sound of water lapping under the balcony, fish plopping and the fluting notes of tropical wading birds. Waking early to the astonishingly noisy croak of a male bull frog which had hopped on to the wooden slat of a blind, I opened a shutter to dislodge him and looked out on to the sky lightening over a strange floating world. In these waters lives the *manjuari*, a very ancient creature, half fish and half alligator which at present is under a strict conservation order. (The small boat tied to the post of the cabin was for braver spirits than mine).

At breakfast I had my first introduction to the juicy fruit of the bomba tree before a walk to a small islet now used as an open-air museum. Here a strangely lifelike scene has been reconstructed by sculptors and archaeologists to illustrate the primitive Indian cultures. Life-size stone figures of men and women fish the lagoons, cook the food, make clay pots, fashion weapons or relax naked surrounded by their children as in life. The tropical plant and bird life of the islet is full of life. Only the stone figures stay still for ever.

Later I had a conversation with a seventeen-year-old teacher at a local school in the marsh country whom I met at the rest centre. She told me of the sad days of her father, a carbon worker, when he was ill with no work and no unemployment benefit. He died soon after the victory of the revolution but it was a comfort to her that he had lived to see that victory. She told me to read the legend beneath the photographic charts on the wall because she said, 'I know it to be true. I have seen it in my own family.' The story read: 'This is a history of a marsh situated in the south of a green island. A marsh that knew only its unhealthy coast, its swamps, its lack of communication and its wretched exploitation of carbon, mean cottages of the fishermen and barefoot swollen-bellied children with mothers old before their time – a marsh called Zapata. We cut a way into the Zapata Swamp about January 1959 . . . Over the forgotten waters of the lagoons emerged a new city of fantasy, returned now to workers to whom it belongs for the use of the people of the whole island and to bring new wealth to the marshes. Those who conceived the plan found the fen without schools, doctors or lights. The revolution sent in teams of technicians. The old latisfundia is now a rice farm. There are clinics for the people and a school with a dining-room . . . ' Elsewhere was the slogan: 'When the people are armed then it can truly be said government by the people has been established.'

Torrential rain, thunder and lightning pounded earth and water for the rest of our stay, so that even the mosquitos that plague this coast were washed away. As we left, sun once more glistened on the drenched vegetation, the flamboyant trees in brilliant flower and the weird aerial roots of the mangroves. White pelicans stood on the banks watching our departure as the ferry took us off into the lagoon. I confess to being completely mesmerised by the eerie beauty of the place which left a melancholy thought: how easily the rot could set in and all human inventiveness be swallowed up as the marsh once more took over (Plate XII).

IN LAS VILLAS:
ANCIENT AND MODERN

CIENFUEGOS IN Las Villas Province, scene of Che Guevara's triumphant campaign, was our next stopping point. It was here in the 'City of a Hundred Fires' that dissension in Batista's armed forces first came into the open when on September 5th 1957 sailors of the naval district joined with the 26th July underground movement in what was to have been a general uprising in Cuba's main ports but in fact only took place on any scale in Cienfuegos. One of its leaders later described how 'The people were out on the streets with the rebels in possession of Cienfuegos' having seized the naval police and the national police headquarters and distributed their stock of arms. But failure of plans elsewhere enabled Batista to concentrate troops and air force on the city and after the bombing of the naval base, rebel positions were overcome one by one.

Today the city is proud of its past while taking a leap forward as an industrial centre of the future. Its concentration of industry clearly demonstrated the way in which, following an early period of trial and error, Cuba's industrial development has now been firmly geared to the needs of agriculture.

On the harbour today stands the Tricontinental Sugar Plant, a completely mechanised sugar loading dock and granary. Rail cars and motor trucks bring the sugar from the great sugar-producing areas of Las Villas Province and dump it on conveyor belts which transfer it to the storehouse. From there the mountain of sugar is dropped unbagged into the holds of ships from Europe, Japan, Russia and elsewhere. Previously much of this work was done by hand. The sugar plant is part of a new industrial zone which includes a fertiliser plant from Britain, part of a completely new

162

chemical industry; a fishing terminal constructed with Soviet help; a large cement factory built in cooperation with the German Democratic Republic to help meet Cuba's acute shortage of cement and in addition the zone includes new flour mills and canning factories.

The neighbourhood organisations see to it that newcomers are involved in community activity and helped to adjust to life in the new towns. Valuable lessons were learnt nationally from the vandalism following the first rehousing schemes in Havana over a decade ago when tenants from the city's worst slums were moved to new fully-equipped apartments. Now, I was told, citizens are drawn at an early age into planning and helping to construct their own amenities which are then better appreciated and cared for. Educational and cultural development is endeavouring to keep pace with industrial growth. Cienfuegos has acquired a new teacher's training school, a technical college and, with UNESCO's aid, an important multi-purpose adult education centre.

It was in Cienfuegos incidentally that I had my first contacts with Cuban amateur dramatics in a play written and produced by the workers of the Tricontinental Sugar Plant, entitled *The Ferment – a history of a sugar mill*, one of three plays to receive awards in the region for work written and performed by amateur theatre groups.

When time has stood still

Both Cienfuegos and Trinidad are ancient Cuban towns built by the Spanish in 1514 on the south coast of Las Villas but today there could be no greater contrast than between the two. While Cienfuegos with its population growth and modern industrial development is rushing forward into the future, Trinidad is a city where time seems to have stood still. Two hundred years ago, it was one of the wealthiest cities in Hispanic America. Men who accompanied Hernan Cortez in his conquest of Mexico walked down its cobbled streets and Cortez himself lived here soon after the city was founded by Diego Velasquez (Plate XVI).

The surrounding Escambray region is being developed as a milk and beef production area. Dairies, reservoirs, factories, schools built by local people are part of a plan for seven new towns but when we arrived at the ancient Cuban city, the Escambray mountains were half hidden in mist and their quiet undisturbed. My diary notes written at 7 p.m. on the first evening record: 'Slept after the journey and woke just in time to see the last of a luminous sunset. Looked out from the balcony on the great semi-circle of the bay, the pallid curve of the water with, on each side, the dark mountains. The light from the room is attracting great moths, very handsome with grey-striped bodies and orange wings. This motel is a little two-roomed house of white-washed stone with a high-walled patio – all very pleasing and simple. Carlos and driver are immediately next door. The tact with which I am given quiet to be on my own as well as receiving every help when needed is a great boon.'

The evening meal in Trinidad city was taken in what is known as the Cave restaurant built in rock over a huge cave. Here it was a pleasure to see Cuban family parties enjoying what was presumably a holiday weekend. I remember the meal mainly on account of a reply from Carlos to my comment that Cuban fathers seem to enjoy the company of their children. His remarks were particularly interesting coming from a man: 'Cuban fathers have always been fond of their children. Fondness for children is a well-known Cuban characteristic. But for fathers to care for their children in the sense of doing their washing or seeing after them in other domestic ways, that is another matter and something that is very slow in coming. The next revolution I think will have to be a woman's revolution for a place in society which is her own right. The eight-hour day will have to force a change. There is too much myth connected with women. First she is a woman then she is a married woman and a 'wife' and then a 'mother' and this myth of wife and mother works too much for the benefit of the man. There have been big advances since the Revolution but the old man-made society with its laws made for men by men is a long time a-dying.' Both our

164

driver and Carlos were men from Oriente 'where all the best people came from' they laughingly claimed, but throughout the period leading up to 1959 Carlos was working in Havana. Love for Cuba and pride in its achievements obviously ran very deep. At the same time I found our conversations all the more valuable because these Cubans took an unblinkered view of the complex problems facing revolutionary movements in Cuba and the world.

Morning in old Trinidad's main plaza confirmed the city's reputation as one of the finest living examples of ancient Hispanic architecture. Its streets are said to be paved by stones used as ballast in the Spanish galleons when they came to fetch the island's coffee, sugar and tobacco. The Cuban Tourist Commission INIT has declared the whole centre of the town a national monument. Everything in this part of the city has been kept in harmony with the tone set by the old manor houses with their moorish, red-tiled roofs, unadorned facades, wide doors and carved wooden window grills. Extensive restoration work is in progress and in the city museum we watched two young girls trained in the art skilfully retouching the surprised eyebrows of Cuba's oldest wooden saint. Other museums will be created in Trinidad's colonial palaces. one to collate the natural history of the Escambray mountains, one to house the documents and visually recreate the region's revolutionary history and another to display a diversity of local crafts.

Living examples of local craftsmanship could be seen in a room converted by the Ministry of Light Industry into a small workshop. Here women workers were plaiting the intricate patterns of the traditional straw hat or *sombrero* (Plate XIII). Elder women passed on their skills to younger ones who worked an eight-hour day for eighty pesos (eighty dollars) a month. Most of the women we talked to had never worked outside their houses before and were obviously enjoying the new companionship. As we talked, a donkey clip-clopped across the sunny square as it might have done centuries ago except that then the upper section of the square was strictly reserved for the promenade of the Spanish aristocracy and no donkey would have dared set foot in it, however daintily.

Teacher training on a mountain top

A memorable event during the stay in Las Villas was a visit to a teacher training college in the mountains at Topes de Collantes. The journey on the mountain bus was full of interesting sidelights on everyday life in Las Villas Province. Due to a breakdown, there was a two-hour wait at the bus terminus in Trinidad which was crammed with people of all ages a few of whom had been waiting all night. Two factors my guide explained coincided to form a bottleneck in long distance transport. On the one hand the big movement between town and country with everyone feeling the urge to visit relatives, and, on the other hand, the effect of the U.S. embargo on supply of spare parts and immigration of skilled mechanics. British Leyland buses were in evidence but even here there have been problems. A crash programme to assemble and deliver buses in record time was beginning to take effect but clearly lack of transport was still causing considerable hardship as could be seen in the consternation on people's faces when a bus arrived and there was insufficient room for all, an event that admittedly rarely occured as seats appeared to have been booked previously. Immediately round us in the waiting-room was an elderly man returning home from a hospital visit to his mountain village where, according to him, before the revolution there had been no bus at all; a woman accompanied by her husband who had just had her pregnancy confirmed and was pleased about it; a young army man going home on leave; a woman in her early twenties with seven children, and a couple with their first baby whose father I noticed coped with getting the feeding bottle warmed. Apart from the few weary ones who had waited all night, the whole station and the street outside presented a lively scene of animated conversation with much joking and laughter and general tolerance of the situation. Sombreros of the kind we had seen being made were much in evidence with young short-haired farmers cutting a dash in high curved brims and intricate patterns. Once more this crowd made one aware of the sense of colour and design in Cuban clothes despite rationing.

At length our bus arrived. Then came the climb up the forested mountain side with goats and pigs taking to their heels at the sound of our furiously hooting horn. Half way up our engine begins to boil and passengers alight while the driver draws water from the wayside well. Lorries-full of standing workers hail us as they pass and we continue on up the steep hard-surfaced road to a height where the small black vultures are our only neighbours.

Against the skyline the tall building of a former sani-torium built by Batista showed we were arriving at Topes de Collantes. The fresh mountain air was a relief after the heat of the bus as we made our way to the local party office. Here we met geography teacher Ana who had been at the training school for six years. She explained that we were seeing the mountain college in its last term before the transference of its pupils elsewhere and its conversion into a worker's rest centre.

In a way it was the end of an era. On the eve of revolution there were several thousand teachers who, though on the books, were not at work, partly because many of them were townspeople loth to work in the countryside where amenities were so few compared to city life. After the alphabetisation campaign, the revolutionary government threw out a challenge to young people to train as teachers in rural areas. To help those who had lived all their lives in towns to accustom themselves to the conditions of their future life, two teacher-training schools were organised in the mountains followed by the final course in Havana. For the first year, students went to a camp at Minas del Frio in the mountains in Oriente where conditions were really spartan but where the area with its associations appealed to youth as a challenge and an adventure. This was followed by a year's study here at Topes de Collantes in the Escambray mountains where the former large sanatorium provided readily available hostel accommodation. By the end of the 1960s the school community numbered over seven thousand students, with about four hundred teachers as well as administrative staff and construction workers.

Two research groups were using this mountain top community as a centre at the time of my visit. One was an educational research team and the other a theatre workshop group whose members shared and studied the everyday life of the country people, wrote plays based on this experience and gave performances in the villages inviting criticism and participation from their audiences. I was not able to meet the educational researchers but their programme sounded interesting. Educationalists in Cuba have been looking into questions of wide relevance such as imagination and its development in the pre-school age; the development of the logical faculty in children's thinking; psychological aspects of learning from machines; causes of drop-outs in teacher-training schools, and new ways of evaluating school education.

By the 'seventies, it was felt the original aims of the mountain teacher-training schools had been achieved. They have now been replaced by training colleges in the regions nearer the students' homes and in 1973-4 students from Topes de Collantes transferred to the new teacher-training institute for primary school teachers in Cienfuegos, built to house a thousand students of whom at present seven hundred and twenty-one are girls and three hundred and thirty-one boys. A total of twenty-three subjects are offered with professional subjects including educational theory and practice, Marxism, psychology and art education. Fourth and fifth year students take teaching practice in the primary schools of the city while third year students observe classes in a primary school annex of the institute. Science laboratories, carpenter's shop, metal and ceramics and art and music studios, barbers and hairdressers, gymnastics and sports facilities all form part of the new college campus. Students enter at about twelve, after a full primary school education and graduate as primary school teachers at the early age of sixteen or seventeen years to meet Cuba's urgent needs. However, future plans visualise the age and educational level required of entrants being raised to twelfth grade which will turn teacher training into a university level career.

FARMING IN CAMAGÜEY

CIEGO DE Avila was our centre during the stay in Camagüey Province, the great sugar and milk producing area of Cuba.

A sugar town

Not far from Ciego de Avila is the Central Venuezela, one of the island's five largest sugar mills and now the centre of a developing sugar town. Tree-lined roads of small modern houses surround the mill and almost at the gate is a new nursery school and a children's playground. It was Militia Day and groups of workers in militia caps were talking at the entrance at the hour of our interview with the mill committee. This took place in a room just large enough to hold the ten of us, the works management committee typically consisting of representatives of mill organisations including the Communist Party, the Young Communists and the Union together with the manager and chief of personnel.

'We want to help you all we can to make it a good book,' said José Manuel, a worker with long years in the industry, 'so ask us anything you like about the mill.' This was an opportunity not to be missed and from the wealth of their combined experience I learnt the following:

The mill was one of those nationalised in 1960. Previously it was owned by the Atlantic Gulf Company who besides owning every piece of land in the area, owned the railway, the local police and the shops. At one time some mills even minted their own coin. Essential mill workers lived in tied cottages owned by the mill and if a worker died, the family lost both house and breadwinner. Before the revolution, it was easy for the company to find the extra cane cutters they needed during harvest because the majority of sugar-field workers had regular employment for about only three or four months of the year and in addition until the 1940s boat loads of casual workers were brought in from Haiti and elsewhere. Because there were always plenty of hungry cane cutters, the field workers were unprotected but the mill workers were skilled men and the unions managed to get better protection for them. One particularly progressive measure they succeeded in obtaining was a fixed wage for mill workers even during what was known as the dead season after harvest is finished. Because of this privileged position the mill owners tried to create among mill maintenance men a kind of aristocracy of labour so as to divide and weaken the men.

When the capitalists left they took out of Cuba not only money but skilled people – so the immediate task within the industry, I was told, was to improve skills and train new people. To this end there was a national plan for those with long experience in the industry to pass on their knowledge to the younger generation and one of the biggest technical schools in the province was built next to the mill. Before there had been a small elementary school. Now there was a big new primary school and a secondary school near at hand. A hundred and fifty workers in the Central Venuezela were at the time attending adult education classes and through the worker-peasant faculties some had passed on to university courses. At the same time, the mill itself became a school where students learnt practical skills from the workers and applied their research.

During harvest time Central Venuezela employed more than two thousand workers. I noticed new houses were being built in the mill village and was interested to know how they were allocated since I knew the housing shortage was so acute that many young couples had to live with their parents as they do in our own country. One of the union men explained that a general assembly was first called at which applications and proposals were invited. Then the local authority and representatives of local organisations visited house by house to inspect conditions. This was followed by another general meeting with further discussion, if priorities were not clear in which, person by person, each was asked their opinion.

Lessons learnt

The union secretary went on to explain that since 1970 there had been a very necessary strengthening of the role of the trade unions. 'Naturally when the workers own the mill as we do, the trade union's function is different from what it was when the capitalists owned it. Looking after workers' wages and conditions is still very important but the union is also much concerned with increasing production and safeguarding the Revolution.' In the first years after victory individual unions had been merged into one union of all workers but recently individual unions for each industry had been rehabilitated. Then came the great testing time of the 1970 sugar harvest – 'the Moncada of the Ten Millions' – when the whole nation was mobilised to reach the very high target the country had set itself and towards which the Central Venuezela processed thousands of tons of sugar.

We did not discuss the matter but a tremendous concentration of energy and enthusiasm had gone into the effort and there must have been bitter disappointment in this mill and every mill in Cuba, when the harvest fell short of the much publicised target even though the 1970 harvest was the biggest in history. But lessons of the utmost importance to Cuba's future were learnt by the setback.

Fidel Castro in a strongly self-critical speech before thousands in Revolution Square and before the world, analysed the imbalance in the economy caused by over-straining for the sugar target in order to raise Cuba's purchasing power.

'Above all,' he said, 'we want the people to understand ... because our problems will not be solved by means of miracles performed by individuals. Only the people can perform miracles ... We are going to begin by pointing out the responsibility that all of us, and in particular I, have for these problems ... I believe that we, the leaders of the Revolution, have cost the people too much in our process of learning.' Speaking on behalf of the Government, the Cuban Prime Minister then called for union meetings at grass roots level in every place of work in order to review the grave problems facing the economy, followed by assemblies of workers within each industry to pass their opinions to ministries, culminating in a national congress of workers.

Making the sugar

At the time of the visit, the mill machinery was being overhauled for the next harvest so I was disappointed in not being able to see the sugar-making process for myself. However the next best thing was to have it explained to me by mill workers themselves as we walked through the old mill and the new. Cane, I was told, must not lie on the field because the juice dries and the acid content rises. Cranes therefore pick up the canes and dump them in huge iron cages mounted on trucks for delivery to the mill. Here the cane is chopped and smashed on the rollers so that the juice runs out into huge funnels. The treacle left after the sugar crystallises used to be thrown away but is now used for cattle feed, for the manufacture of alcohol and for growing yeasts. Furnaces in the mill are mostly run on the dried cane left after the juice has run out.

Twentieth-century mechanisation has transformed working conditions and methods but fundamentally the process itself is not very different from the small primitive mills of the 1860s as described by a one time sugar slave, Esteban Montejo. Then there were three boilers, big copper ones with wide mouths. The first cooked the juice, in the next the froth was taken off, and in the third the treacle was boiled until ready. Then the treacle was poured into a trough and tipped into a sugar locker where the raw sugar was left to drain. Once the sugar had cooled boys went in bare feet with spade and shovel and a handbarrow to carry it away to the stacking sheds.

Across the road from the mill, the technical school for intermediate sugar technicians was showing an exhibition of students' work. Among the students to whom we spoke, some were making spare parts for the mill. Twenty-two of the students were women, a number that was expected to increase greatly when the school was in full swing. At the time, there were a hundred and twenty-nine women working in the mill but this number too was expected to increase with improved facilities. Technical institutes and schools like this one are being built next door to all Cuba's main sugar mills as part of the work-study partnership.

A *celebration*

The date of our visit coinciding with Militia Day meant that we were invited to a little celebration that evening when certificates were presented to local members, women and men who had served in the militia for twelve years – the full term of its existence. I was both surprised and moved to be asked by the mill workers in a gesture of friendship to present the first few of these certificates. The ceremony was a simple family affair, on the surface not unlike past homeguard events in village halls at home. There were many women militia members and from time to time toddlers clambered on and off the platform as parents and elder brothers and sisters came up to receive their certificates. As my interpreter said – these were the sole but precious reward for all the hours spent guarding Cuba during the past twelve hard years. The warm reception in this sugar mill town for a visitor from England illustrated once more the genuine and spontaneous friendship of the citizens of this island for friendly people of all nations – a characteristic that has led the Cubans, despite their own conditions of scarcity, to be among the first to rush aid to disaster areas, whether to Honduras, Peru, Vietnam or Nicaragua.

Mechanising the sugar harvest

Traditionally sugar cane has been handcut by the cane cutter armed with a machete, an exhausting job that absorbs many labour hours. The machine that will increasingly mechanise this work was demonstrated to us during a visit to the National Training Institute for Agricultural Mechanics where the average age of the staff was twenty-five years. Here we met four young men whose enthusiasm was evident for work which was largely new to Cuba's experience. They explained that one of the hardest tasks the revolution had to face was the technological backwardness of underdevelopment. Soon after victory, a serious labour shortage made mechanisation doubly urgent but lack of knowledge at first put the precious machinery at risk, maintenance being of special importance in an eroding climate.

The machine shop was obviously an object of some pride. Here beside the rice and cotton harvesters was a sugar cane combine harvester. The young Cubans explained that while rice was now fully mechanised, the invention of a satisfactory cane cutter had proved one of the most knotty problems. Cane unlike maize and rice, tends to lie down, particularly if the sugar content is high, when the wind will entangle and flatten it, while on bumpy ground the machine cuts sometimes too high, sometimes too low. After many trials with adaptations of Australian and Soviet models, mass production of the Soviet combine harvester has now been decided upon, combined with planting on pre-conditioned and suitable ground.

Today a Cuban plant is being built which will enable Cuba for the first time to mass produce her own sugar cane harvesters. This is a very big breakthrough. The machine industry, like the chemical industry, was practically non-existent before 1959 and successful mechanisation could reduce the three hundred and seventy thousand cane cutters used at harvest to fifty thousand. This would release workers to re-train for other and less gruelling work, and there is no fear that mechanisation would bring unemployment in modern Cuba (Plate XIV).

Acres upon acres of Camagüey Province are covered by pale green stretches of sugar cane all of which, when it ripens in January, must be swiftly and efficiently harvested to prevent spoilage. The province's population (nine hundred thousand in the early 'seventies) has always been unevenly spread so that many rural areas are thinly populated. With the disappearance of a pool of rural unemployed in the first years of the revolution, cane cutting became one of the main tasks of the army, but in the late 'sixties the problem of helping the small regular work force was handed over to the youth organisations to solve and out of this grew the idea of the Centennial Youth Columns formed in 1968 to celebrate a hundred years of independence struggles. An appeal was launched for youth of both sexes of sixteen years upward not engaged in full time study to devote three years to helping the economy in agriculture, in industry and at sea with the fishing fleet. During this period they would complete their compulsory military training and, as well as giving a boost to the economy, the idea was to give young people the experience of creating a community of their own age group while doing a challenging task that would bring them in close touch with working people and the realities of life. Of the first volunteers, twenty-four thousand stayed the course, there being a smaller drop-out of girls than boys.

In 1970, Year of the Ten Million, the columns had the highest production record in all Cuba and many cane cutters who earned the title of Hero of Work came from the Youth Columns. I learnt all this and much more from twenty-one-year-old Enrique and twenty-year-old Pedro of the Youth Columns' General Staff. They explained that many volunteers when they first arrived had a low educational level (first to sixth grade primary) so the aim was to include regular daily periods of general classes in order to create a habit of study that would continue in later life. In a way the columns formed part of Cuba's Parallel System of Education which picked up adolescents who had dropped out or fallen behind in regular schooling and gave them a second opportunity. I was taken to a small museum resplendent with trophies and photographs of the brigades and here I was shown the record of Leonardo Mendozo, nicknamed Mochita, four feet and three-quarters in height and national Hero of Work who broke all records by cutting three hundred thousand arrobas of cane in a hundred and eighty-three days (one arroba equals about eleven kilos). He wanted to remain working in cane but was persuaded to go to a school for agricultural mechanics because 'the first duty of young people is to become skilled'.

We talked about the ideas behind Cuba's educational revolution and the need for people to develop and change in the process of changing society. Enrique put it this way: 'I can only speak in relation to my work in the rather special case of the Youth Columns. When a boy or girl joins the columns, they declare their willingness to forgo all material incentives other than a just share of social benefits and to work solely for the satisfaction of fulfilling a task that our country needs them to do. This develops a feeling for the collective – a feeling of us all being in it together. It entails no extra hardship to families because food and all necessities are covered and a monthly allowance is made to families of columnists according to need.'

Pedro developed his colleague's points more generally: 'In Cuba we want boys and girls from an early age to know about social problems not only in our country but in the whole of Latin America. From childhood too, we stress the importance of study because one's educational level is a component of one's freedom. As Martí said, an educated people is a free people. But from the beginning we try to give children the idea that it is as important to help others as to improve themselves. Then, very important for the new society, there must be in everyone a love of work because only through work can we create the material base that one day will provide sufficient of everything to give to everyone what they really need regardless of how much they can contribute. Right now it is scarcity and underdevelopment

177

that we are fighting to overcome and in that battle the Youth Columns have their part to play.'

Evening in Camagüey Province was spent with girl columnists whose brigade had just finished the fruit harvest. The camp, a permanent one with its own small sanatorium, was almost empty. All except twenty of the brigade of a hundred and fifty were away on leave for the regular week's home visit following two month's work and the rest were at a rehearsal of a Molière play that they were entering for a drama festival.

Our three companions were Ana, Maria and Blasa and this time there was leisure for more personal talk. Ana from Havana wanted to work in army communications when she left the columns. Her parents were divorced and she had no previous experience of productive work but found life with the columns more stimulating than being at home. The work she liked best was driving a tractor and one of her pleasantest memories was the day when the column was presented with a gun for the highest production. Nineteen-year-old Maria was from farming stock near Santiago de Cuba. Both she and her fiancé whom she had met at a party in the camp wanted to continue to farm in the area and she wished to become a tractor driver. Blasa had reached first grade of secondary school, a higher grade than the others, when she joined the brigade three years ago. She was now twenty and was remaining in the camp for another year to continue her job as political instructor. We asked what this entailed and were told it involved leading discussions on current events and 'generally explaining Marxist ideas'. Her mother was active in the Federation of Cuban Women and she herself was going to a political school when she left the columns. Of course, she explained, politics was only one subject in a programme of general studies for which there was a full-time teacher. For women as for men, militia training was part of the course. Blasa told us the columns provided much of their own entertainment and she had in fact met her fiancé when she was called upon to chair a debate between their two brigades which he had helped to organise. The columns had their own music groups (The Beatles' music incidentally was popular in Cuba but their hair styles were not imitated, most men of all ages wearing their hair short).

All except three of the girls who enrolled with the brigade had stayed the full three years and this experience would count as an important testimonial for a career and further study for many who otherwise would have dropped out of education at an early stage.

(The Youth Columns are now part of what is known as the Army of Working Youth under the general direction of the Revolutionary Armed Forces.)

The Dairy Triangle of Camagüey

Ever since the Spanish first brought cattle and horses to Cuba, the rolling plains of Camagüey have been the scene of mounted cowboys rounding up droves of cattle. At first the stock were commonly owned but in more recent times they belonged to proprietors of the vast ranches into which the land was divided. Farmers on horseback are still a feature of the landscape for today a large scale state enterprise known as the Dairy Triangle extends over the grasslands of Camagüey. Milk has been very scarce in Cuba. The position is now improving and when this scheme reaches full production over a period of ten years, it will be stocked by over a million cows. To house the workers needed for this big concern a new town for several thousand is being built with necessary amenities including an agricultural technical institute and new schools.

Chief interest for me was in meeting Cuba's first modern dairy maids, many of them from the Youth Columns, who were handling the fully mechanised milk parlours at a salary of a hundred and six pesos a month. In this work, women are playing a decisive role and their responsibility includes, besides the expensive machinery, the care of calves and calving. The girls we spoke with seemed to be greatly en-

179

joying the work. They pointed out that some of the cows were the first generation offspring of a cross between the native Zebu cow and the pedigree Holstein bull imported from Denmark and it is hoped they will combine the mother's ability to stand the long dry season (November-April) with the Holstein's high milk yield. So far results were quite promising as the milk yield charts showed.

As well as their own speciality, the girls were taking lessons in general subjects in order to raise their educational levels. A class teacher from the columns had mentioned to us how important it was to remove the lack of confidence and embarrassment caused by past educational failure. Now these girls were discovering fresh skills that society urgently needed and breaking entirely new ground in Cuba. When later I read that fifteen miles from Camagüey a new agricultural college had opened and that among its first intake were twenty-two women students studying cattle breeding and fifteen more specialising in the veterinary sciences, I wondered how many of our friends of the Dairy Triangle were among the number (Plate XIII).

Life on a pineapple farm

Our final expedition in Camagüey to a pineapple plantation was impressed on my memory by a meeting with sixty-five-year-old farmworker Manuelo Pedson. At the edge of the pineapple fields, banana, mango and avocado pear trees made a shade round Manuelo's house. We had called unannounced and I remember on our arrival his wife was in the middle of preparing a meal in a roomy kitchen where a sewing machine had recently been in use. It looked on to the back garden where there were pigs and chickens as well as coffee bushes and a patch of beans and root vegetables under the shade of an orange tree.

We talked over a copious supply of fruit juice, sitting in the traditional Spanish rocking chairs that furnished the front room. Manuelo had been in pineapples for over thirty years and was still working at sixty-five. He had two children and two grandchildren and it was noticeable that the first information he volunteered was that both his grandchildren had passed their sixth grade at school. He introduced us to his grandson of thirteen years who wanted to train as an aircraft mechanic and his granddaughter aged twelve years who was going to study English and Russian. Manuelo then answered my questions about the difference the revolution had made to his own life. One big change, he said, was that life was made easier since some of the hard jobs were mechanised and there was a regular wage and full-time work. Almost immediately however, he returned to the question of education – and obviously for him this is what mattered most of all. (The American sociologist, Lowry Nelson, found thirty years ago an immense hunger for education among isolated farming communities).

Manuelo told us that there was no school at all within reach in his boyhood and that he had taught himself to read and write because he wanted to work as a mechanic. He saw an advertisement for a correspondence course and wrote off for details but it was too hard to tackle on his own.

'Right now I want to learn,' he said concentrating his gaze on us as though willing us to understand, 'but I feel it is too hard to begin at my age. I am always telling my grandchildren about it, telling them what a good thing it is to learn with the help of others but on your own – it is very hard.'

We were joined by their daughter who at present worked at a local plant making protective clothing. There was no industry she told us before someone had this simple useful idea. As a child her father was so anxious for her to learn that he searched for a private teacher whom he paid to come to the house but every time she took a test, she had to travel to Camagüey and pay a heavy entrance fee. She reached second year at a higher education institute but her health broke down. Her husband was a driver so with her work in the factory and on top of that her work in the house her life was very full. If she felt stronger next year her intention was to train as a teacher.

This pineapple plantation formed part of the Ministry of Agriculture's Pineapple Plan. It was worked by some two hundred permanent farm workers like Manuelo and helped by technicians from the University of Las Villas and over three hundred members of the Youth Columns. Pineapples need skill and gentle handling so amateur labour can present problems. Rainfall is less important than for some other crops, particularly in the case of the most commonly grown Spanish variety which is resistant to the dry season, but shortage of seed was causing some serious holdups and for this reason one experimental field was concentrating on producing different types of pineapple for seed so that Cuba could build up her own seed stocks and breed new varieties.

IN ORIENTE,
CRADLE OF THE REVOLUTION

ON CROSSING the border into Oriente at 10 a.m. on a Friday morning all three of us fell silent each with our separate thoughts. For the two Cubans this was home country packed with memories. For me it was a province long imagined taking on flesh at last. *Oriente, Scene of the Revolution,* states the border sign. This eastern province is still clearly very much the territory of the peasant farmer as it has been throughout most of Cuba's history. Even when slave labour produced the bulk of Cuba's material goods, in the eastern provinces, and particularly in Oriente, there was, in contrast to most of the rest of the island, a peasant class of independent small farmers working the land with their own hands and it was precisely in these eastern provinces of Oriente, Camagüey and Las Villas that the wars of independence found their main support. Until the agrarian reform measures after 1959, those farmers who owned no land either rented it or, as sharecroppers, handed over half their crop in lieu of rent or scraped a living by squatters' rights.

Today as the road runs further east banana and coconut plantations increase and small individual farms become more frequent, growing for home consumption sweet potatoes, melons, beans, yucca, mango and guava, with coffee covering the hillsides. Glimpses of the very new and the very old flash by us: an artificial insemination centre, numerous tumble-down shacks, tiled roofs of new single-storied houses beside the thatched roofs of cottages, a house cow grazing by the roadside and a boy driving an ox laden with green bananas, children in neat school uniform pouring out of school at noon, a young woman driving a tractor and a hoarding announcing the First Congress of Medicos.

From the balcony of the Hotel Patallo in Holguin one sees

183

the circular sweep of the hills, the highest marked with an ancient pilgrims' cross. On the outer edge of the city, considerable clearance has been made of the derelict shanty town which for centuries fringed the city. More centrally, standing out against the curved tiles of the Spanish period, are the modern buildings of the large hospital donated by the Soviet Union during the devastation caused by Hurricane Flora. According to the Minister of Health's report for 1974, Cuba now has 4.8 hospital beds and one doctor to every thousand inhabitants while each member of the population has five doctor's appointments a year. About half of Cuba's doctors – some three thousand – left the country after the revolution of 1959 and medical equipment which came almost entirely from the United States was cut off by the embargo. Nevertheless, since 1959, the Ministry has trained thirty-four thousand nurses and other health workers as well as over eight thousand doctors.

The only major hospital I visited while in Cuba was one for the mentally sick – the Psychiatric Hospital of Havana which has earned an international reputation. In pre-revolutionary times this was a deplorable place, as photographic records show, where five thousand mental patients lived in degrading conditions: it was first built in 1850 as an asylum for slaves. Now it has been rebuilt into what looks like a small green garden city with an adult occupational centre.

Its director, a bearded ex-guerrilla and doctor in the Rebel Army, believes much of its success is due to many small things that together provide a soothing environment, avoiding friction and creating confidence and hope. The aim is gradually to bring the patients back nearer to society and make them feel that they too belong and are needed. Here the Marxist-Leninist conception of work as something useful to others plays a part, but the emphasis is on work as part of the healing process – something that the patients require for stimulation and involvement. We saw patients cultivating roses for sale and others operating one of the most successful poultry farms in Cuba. A small wage was paid according to work done so as further to create interest. There was a baseball field lit for night play, and a theatre and art studios for the therapeutic use of music, dance and painting. Rocking chairs were much in evidence in numerous small leisure rooms and terraces. There were also hairdressing saloons and mirrors in the houses. In short one was aware throughout of a practical emphasis on the right of each human being to dignity and self respect. The hospital was not full to capacity and there had never been a waiting list, but how far this is typical of provision for mental health in Cuba generally I am unable to say.

Conversation in Holguin

It was in Holguin that I had a discussion with a parent who had decided to send his child to a day primary school rather than to the weekly boarding school offering special facilities for physical training and swimming used by some of his colleagues. He was clearly a staunch revolutionary and I found his ideas of particular interest in relation to a comment by the prominent Soviet psychologist, V. N. Kolbanosvsky, in a recent debate on the family in the journal *Novy Mir*, to the effect that it was important to ensure that the benefits of communal upbringing 'in no way implied that the family is to be alienated from the process of rearing children'.

This particular parent lived in the city and felt that both parents and young children gained from daily contacts. (Obviously the same yardstick could not be applied to isolated rural areas in special cases.) He agreed it was essential to trust young people with great responsibility but he thought the extreme youth of many teachers had its difficulties as well as its advantages and made the role of the parent more important. However he stressed that the revolutionary government was well aware of these problems and had taken careful organisational steps to ensure maximum contact between school and home by involving parents at every stage of school life. For instance there exists a 'Mothers and Fathers for Education' scheme through which parents make it their business to give practical help to the schools while the excellent facilities of the new countryside schools are used by the families of pupils as holiday centres (Plate XIX).

I learnt from the Ministry of Education that it is in fact Ministry policy that children of primary school age should attend day school as it was felt children of this age needed to be with their family. Of 1,899,266 primary school children in 1974, 47,000 were at boarding school and these were there for special reasons such as having no parents, etc.

A primary school prospectus I was given sets down in black and white the parent-school relationship. Before the new school is opened, the parents and local people's organisations are called to a meeting to discuss the general aim of the school and elect representatives to the executive council. After pupils and teachers have met to draw up rules, these are reported to a special meeting of parents. Teachers and parents then continue to meet monthly to discuss their children's progress and where children are experiencing difficulty, the teacher visits the parents to find out if there are social or emotional problems.

In the new weekly-boarding schools for secondary pupils the aim is to create a close involvement between parents, the local community and the school so that Cuban children may benefit from all three in a form that meets the needs of Cuba's population distribution and the present phase of her development.

Care of the pre-school child

I found Dr Miranda, head of the Children's Institute, had the matters we had been discussing very much in mind. Her department now coordinates all work connected with children of pre-school age which she described as a very sensitive area of work in which one had to tread warily. In

186

response to many needs, the Federation of Cuban Women has been the driving force behind big developments in the provision of day-care centres for toddlers from the age of forty-five days upwards. Dr Miranda told me some research was being carried out into the comparative development of Cuban children who attended pre-school groups and those who did not and so far results were very favourable to the former, though there were many factors entering into the comparison that needed sorting out. I was interested to see when visiting a children's circle (as the day-care centres are called) that a psychology student was spending time with newcomers and noting how they were reacting. In the small nursery crèche there were four babies to one helper making constant individual attention possible. To facilitate this, playing and resting space was raised up towards adult level. I noticed quite small babies intrigued with each other as well as with the moving objects round them. Full records for the children included such home background details as whether or not they shared a bed at home with others. Standards of hygiene seemed high as they need to be in a tropical climate where all feeding utensils have to be boiled between meals. Volunteers were helping to meet the obvious shortage of play equipment which, because of the climate cannot be the strenuous outdoor type we are accustomed to.

When I arrived five toddlers at a round table had just finished a meal and it struck me that it must be a great relief to Cuban mothers to know that their children are getting priority for the best balanced diet Cuba can supply. They were all very lively and to a non-specialist seemed full of healthy energy. My only reservation was the very young starting age though I realise one needs to know the special circumstances in every case.

Further visits to day-care centres in 1975 included the beautifully designed and well staffed nursery for a hundred and eighty children of pre-school age at the new town of Alamar, with its own small swimming bath facing the sea, as well as a visit to a fourteen-year-old nursery in Havana. Both showed big improvements in the provision of educational toys and the Cubans in recent years have obviously increasingly drawn upon the long experience of the Soviet Union in pre-school education, adapting it to the Cuban situation. I asked the director at Alamar what she thought of Soviet methods. She considered they were sound as they tended towards smaller groups of similar aged children following a carefully planned time table corresponding to each stage of development which resulted among other things in smoother running. I also asked about the long day for the children away from home. She said the only problem they had found was that there were so many things to do in the centre, the children often cried when they had to leave off what they were doing and go home (Plate X).

In this connection, the comments of a parent I spoke to were interesting. Her three-year-old son had been at one of the less well-equipped infant circles in an adapted private house since he was three months old. She spoke well of the warmth and enthusiasm of the staff and explained how gently the child is introduced to the group life of the day-care centre, particularly when entering between the vulnerable age of six months to two years. Over an adaptation period of five weeks, mother and child both attend at first for one hour only, then gradually the time is extended with the mother staying more and more in the background, in the later stages perhaps disappearing to shop and returning at increasing intervals until the toddler is ready to be left for the whole day. This particular mother works full time as a translator and is also president of the mother's committee of her son's infant circle. Because of being used to group activity and sharing toys from an early age, her little boy enjoys sharing and she finds him very outgoing towards people in general. Although the parents are only with their son in the evenings and weekends, she felt they got the very best out of their time together because they were fresh to enjoy him and, since there was a long mid-day sleep period in the nursery time-table, the child too was still lively in the evenings.

A new training centre will soon lead to the availability of fully qualified nursery staff but at present most helpers are unqualified though all receive regular coaching and refresher courses during working hours.

Much less organised and staff intensive than the infant circles are what are known as 'kindergartens' which have long existed in Cuba. These are play group centres sometimes situated in a small park, with a garden for play, and a simple shelter for free indoor activity under the care of a helper or child minder. One meal is supplied and the children are collected in the afternoon. Future development, however, will be concentrated on the infant circles which are seen as an extension of Cuba's educational system. Cuba now provides six hundred of these day-care centres for over fifty thousand children of pre-school age, in an island whose total population is about the size of Greater London. Meanwhile the Children's Institute is working on a many sided plan in order to build a sound scientific basis on which to improve the mental and physical health of young children. As part of this, for the first time in history, Cuban norms for Cuban children have been drawn up relative to age and development.

From Bayamo to Santiago

The last lap of the journey from west to east of Cuba is studded with place names indelibly linked with the history of the island. There is Bayamo, for instance, where was born the conspiratorial movement against Spain with the formation here in 1867 of the revolutionary committee headed by Carlos Manuel de Céspedes. In the quiet of the morning one could imagine the voice of the 'Father of Cuba' declaring from the mill in La Demajagua the day he signed the declaration of independence. 'This sun you are seeing rise over the Sierra Maestra comes to shine with its glory on freedom in Cuba. Long live Free Cuba.' Bayamo became the capital and seat of the first revolutionary government under the presidency of Manuel de Céspedes after the first major victory over the Spaniards on October 20th 1867 and for the first time here in Bayamo Spaniards and black and white Cubans took part together in municipal government. Here too was published the first independent newspaper *El Cubano Libre* which became the official organ of the revolutionaries. It was in its pages that Cuba's national anthem *Las Bayamese* first appeared. Later when the Spanish counter-attacked and marched in force on Oriente, the defence of Bayamo became impossible and rather than let it fall into the hands of the enemy, the citizens burnt down the town. On January 12th 1869 Bayamo was burnt to ashes.

Just over a hundred years later, in brilliant sunshine, the little town as we passed had a modern air with pleasant new one-storey buildings, some blocks of flats, passengers alighting from a new-looking bus, and an agricultural machinery centre and on the outskirts, a rodeo. Our driver spent his childhood here and both he and my guide agreed that if ever Cuba were invaded, rather than surrender the citizens of Bayamo would once more resort to a scorched earth policy if circumstances required it. Cubans mean it when they say *patria o muerte: venceremos* (a free homeland or death. we will overcome).

Now the road is climbing to Baire in the high mountains. Here the slopes are forested with cocoa plantations and century-old coffee trees stretching to the foothills of the Sierra Maestra. Rivers run in deep gorges and here and there the sun highlights the foliage of the red-leaved shade-trees, the *ceibas* and the grey-leaved *yagrumbas*. Very many of Cuba's precious timber-producing trees were felled for fuel in the years of the sugar boom. Now forestry schools are training foresters for an extensive plan of reafforestation. It was to the south west of our route, at San Lorenzo in the Herreria Sierra that de Céspedes was shot by the Spaniards after disagreement in the revolutionary forces had led to his deposition as president. In a letter to his wife he described the hut where he spent his last days, and among other things taught the peasant children to read. 'My house is large

190

enough,' he wrote. 'It's a palm-thatched one but covered with sturdy boards ... In my room I have a table desk, a hammock, a bench that goes with the table all of cedar; my bag of weapons and other utensils. There is no lack of food and I can take a good bathe in the river. Everyone is very kind ... I still receive the same respect as when I was President. Wherever I go except in official places I am welcomed as before but now it must be more sincere and for that I am grateful.'

Heroic city

'The battle of the economy can be won by the help of all.' This slogan spans the heights overlooking the plain which spreads green mile upon green mile towards Santiago de Cuba – the ancient town nestling against the mountains at the edge of a shining sea.

Santiago de Cuba, capital of Oriente and scene of a century of freedom struggles, was founded across the bay by the Spanish conquistadors in 1514, moving to its present site eight years later. In the older parts of the city there are delightful traces everywhere of the Spanish colonial architecture as well as the influence of the French coffee planters from Haiti. The city is sheltered on two sides by mountains of the Sierra Maestra range and the climate here is more intense than elsewhere in Cuba, the vegetation being particularly lush and tropical.

A pleasing example of modern Cuban architecture is the beautifully sited Hotel Tricontinental built in 1966 for the Tricontinental Conference. But the house that stays in my memory for quite different reasons is a three-roomed house in a narrow street in Santiago de Cuba – the home of twenty-three-year-old teacher Frank País, a son of a Baptist minister, who became leader of the civil resistance movement in Oriente and was known to the underground as Carlos. Around 1955 a particularly active group of Acción Nacional Revolucionaria led by Frank País and Pepito Tey linked up with Fidel Castro and the 26th July Movement and País soon after became the Movement's national coordinator. Those who worked with him remember his talent for organisation combined with an ability to involve many types of people in struggle. When the greatly depleted band of rebels that had landed in *Granma* reached the Sierra Maestra and called for supplies and men, it was Frank País who, with the help of Celia Sanchez Mauduley and others, recruited eighty volunteers from the region for the Rebel Army. Very soon after his younger brother was assassinated, Frank País was shot, in the street outside the house of a friend where he had sought refuge, on the night of July 30th 1957.

The house with its small vine-covered patio remains as a memorial to the resistance leader just as he left it. In his living room is a selection of his pupils' work which he appears to have been correcting at the time of the attack. His mask hanging on the wall is a reminder of his extreme youth and untimely death. My Cuban companions said that the death of Frank País was a particularly great loss for the revolution and the impact of the simple house and personal possessions obviously brought back memories of many others who had paid with their lives in the underground struggle.

The attitude of Cubans to civil resistance in the anti-Batista struggle is similar to that of the people in the occupied countries in the Second World War. They look upon it as an heroic episode in which all forms of struggle, including acts of sabotage, were justified against a brutal fascist regime.

It was from the Professor of History at the University of Santiago de Cuba that I heard reminiscences of the massive strike following the death of Frank País which spread throughout Oriente and far beyond into Camagüey and Las Villas Provinces. During over a hundred years of independence struggles, Santiago has been in the thick of battle and in the nineteen-fifties its links with the Rebel Army in the surrounding mountains were particularly direct. The picture sometimes painted by writers on Cuba of an inert working

192

class in the cities waiting to be fired into action by a small guerrilla grouping in the mountains is particularly wide of the mark in relation to Santiago de Cuba. Certainly the Cubans do not see it this way. One has only to remember the words of Che Guevara speaking in the city on November 30th 1964: 'The martyrs whose deaths we recall today are but links in the long chain of martyrs who died during the two years of revolution in the city of Santiago. Every day men of the people gave their lives here, around this city and in the ranks of the Rebel Army which they swelled with their sons, for the freedom of Cuba.

'We often thought of the dangers faced by the people in the city, of how difficult it must be for a known revolutionary to keep up the clandestine struggle with a permanent death sentence hanging over his or her head. This is why on a night in late July 1957, at the moment when two columns of the Rebel Army were formed, all the officers wrote a letter to Frank País and the City of Santiago thanking them for their heroic, firm and prolonged action in support of the revolutionary struggle. The letter, however, was never received for Frank País gave his life as well in the insurrection against the Batista dictatorship. This city has won the plaudits of a whole nation.'

The University of Oriente

During a meeting with Council members of the Humanities Faculty of the University of Oriente, both staff and students stressed the important part played in Cuba's revolutionary movement by students whose militancy made them a target of the establishment in troublous times stretching right back to the historic shooting of medical students by Spanish authorities in 1871.

Besides one private university, before the revolution there were three state universities: Havana University established in the eighteenth century, Las Villas University in 1952 and the University of Oriente in 1949. On the eve of revolution

193

the universities were closed as they had been since a strike at the end of 1956, but the 1953 census gives numbers of university students as twenty thousand compared with present day figures of fifty thousand (Fidel Castro on November 4th 1974).

Although the University of Oriente was not founded in Santiago until the middle of the twentieth century the city had long served as an intellectual centre where new ideas found an airing. Once established, the university soon attracted academics from abroad of a variety of opinions, among them Spanish intellectuals of left-wing views who emigrated to Cuba in the years following the Spanish Civil War. Even before the revolution, I was told, at this university there were not the usual divisions between academic staff and students. Both were already drawing together in one revolutionary whole, and linking up with the workers in a joint struggle against tyranny. Several of Cuba's revolutionary leaders were reared at Santiago University and teachers' college, Frank País among them.

We discussed the changed role of students in present day Cuba. In the past Cuban universities had followed the general pattern of Latin American universities in seeking autonomy from the state in order to free themselves from the influence of successive repressive oligarchies. (The Cuban Ministry of Education it will be remembered was described by the World Bank Report on Cuba in 1951 as a stronghold of bribery and corruption where numerous unsavoury characters found a niche on the pay roll.) In the new situation created by popular forces taking power in 1959, the position of the universities was altered. Those I spoke to were emphatic that the correct role of the university in revolutionary Cuba was, under the general direction of the Ministry of Education, to help the Government supply the needs of the community by a vast extension and democratisation of education – an aim for which revolutionaries in the university had fought in the past.

There has been a fundamental change in the emphasis of university education. Before 1959, it bore little relation to the needs of the Cuban economy since it was geared to the individual requirements of a small élite. The effect was to produce a situation where in 1952, in an island whose well being depended on agricultural production, there were about ten times more graduate lawyers than there were qualified agronomists and veterinary technicians. The revolutionary government, believing it was essential to bring about a rapid change in bias if Cuba was ever to throw off underdevelopment, attracted students to science and technology by giving more scholarships to these faculties. As a result in the ten years following victory, when the total number of places increased by about a half, the proportion in the humanities dropped considerably while student numbers in the sciences rose steeply. (In Havana University, for instance, where science faculties have been rehoused and extended beyond all recognition on a site outside the city adjoining a state farm, comparative figures of graduates for the year 1972-73 were as follows: Technology 598, Medicine 1129, Agronomy 395, Education 276, Humanities 284, Sciences 536, Economy 62.)

At the University of Oriente as at every level of secondary and higher education the dialogue between work and study is fundamental to Cuba's educational revolution. Universities are paired with farms and factories and other enterprises where students as part of their professional practice spend a proportion of their time (mainly in the fourth and fifth years). As council members put it: 'The dialogue helps us both. Industry gets specialised help with their particular problems as, for instance, when medical students apply their research to health hazards in the mines where a new wing of the university has been built. At the same time the universities feel the immense benefit of a constant link with everyday working life and the satisfaction of seeing one's work of direct value to society. The old ivory tower image is a thing of the past.'

Student allowances if necessary amount to a wage sufficient to support a family. By 1973-74 nearly half of that year's enrollment consisted of workers directly involved in production, the remainder being students taking regular courses and following the work-study programme.

There has, in the last few years in Cuba, been a significant change in the comparative proportion of women university students in the various faculties. 1973 statistics show that in Education 62% were women, Humanities 60.4%, Sciences 50.1%, Medicine 50%, Economics 42.2%, Agricultural Sciences 26.5%, Technology 25.1%. I wondered if these numbers were reflected in the membership of leading committees in the university. The student union secretary replied that when the union was recently reformed in his own faculty there was not a single woman elected on to the executive. Now there was one. Yet in the general activity of the union, he said, the contribution of women students was sometimes greater than that of the men. A member of the teaching staff reminded us that one had to keep in mind the special historical background to these things. Every sphere of life was open now to Cuban women but there was a long way to catch up because four centuries of Spanish colonial rule had kept them cloistered in the home out of public life and for the most part out of production.

A family code

I thought of this conversation two years later when the nearly two million strong Federation of Cuban Women held its second congress on the occasion of its fifth anniversary in 1974. As usual in Cuba, this was an occasion for sober analysis as well as an opportunity for congratulation on the immensely energetic achievements that have won such high respect for the Federation, including the fact that its previous members contributed over ninety-five million hours of voluntary work the previous year. What made the congress an historic occasion was the discussion on the family code, the culmination of a lively debate in street, home and work-place throughout the island. This legislates for equality in the home with shared responsibility for household chores and the care and education of children.

196

In his concluding speech, Prime Minister Fidel Castro asked if Cuba, a socialist country with almost sixteen years of revolution, could really say that Cuban women had acquired full equality in deed as well as word? And he gave figures some of which, he said, really gave cause for concern. Before the revolution, there were 194,000 working women of whom 70% were domestics. Today there are three times that amount working in civilian state employment, representing just over a quarter of the total working force. (Comparable world figure as given by the United Nations is 34%.) 'Nevertheless', said Fidel Castro, 'the number of women holding leadership positions in all this apparatus of production, services and administration is only 15%. Only 12.79% of our Party members are women.' He pointed out a still more indicative figure. The number of women chosen as delegates in local government elections to new organs of people's power was 7.6% and the number of women elected was 3%. Yet women make up half the population and there can be no question but that at every stage of the revolution their contribution has been outstandingly responsible, courageous and self sacrificing.

Fidel Castro also spoke of the need to battle against the superman mentality that resisted the wife going out to work and having a public life of her own. There was applause when he said: 'We don't see why anyone should be frightened because women's equality is being discussed although some were frightened when the discussions on the family code was launched (Laughter). What should really frighten us as revolutionaries is that in reality women still do not have absolute equality in Cuban society because this means we have not completed the Revolution.'

Even in 1971, when getting the economy on its right course was taking up all energy, similar ideas concerning sex equality were being discussed. Vilma Espin, the Federation's president, told me just before I left Cuba that Cubans saw women's full liberation as a task for society as a whole, men and women together. They wanted to avoid the struggle wasting its strength in a war between the sexes which would not get to the social roots of the problem and substituting male slavery for female slavery in the home would solve nothing. More public housekeeping was needed in the form of thousands of laundries, canteens and take-home meals, day-care centres and day boarding schools but, though there had been big improvements, this was a long business in a developing country and working women still had to return home and do a further long stint in the house. The immediate essential need was for a new relationship befitting revolutionaries where men and women shared work both in the home and outside the home as equal partners. This meant clearing away age-old habits of thought that go back to a time in society when women were looked upon as property and as Françoise Fourier, one of the earliest pioneers of women's rights, put it 'fit only to clean pots and pans and mend old pants'. Martí looked forward to a time when 'women would become man's equal not sit as a toy at his feet', but old ideas become so ingrained that for a time, even when building a new society without exploitation, places of authority still tend to be left to men.

Cubans hope the family code that has generated so much discussion, by bringing these prejudices into the open will help both the legal and the educational process of eradicating them, and once more Cuba is providing an example by doing these things in a style all her own.

Retracing history: from Moncada to Sierra

Two memorable journeys to historic places were planned for the last weekend in Santiago, a weekend linked in memory with the great beauty everywhere of Cuba's flowering trees. The blooms of many of these tropical plants are pollinated by birds and bats as well as insects hence their large size to allow of easy entry. On city streets, the sun was still intensely hot, jasmine was in blossom and lilies grew in profusion in a small pond in the garden where we stayed. There were, I remember, pale ones that opened only at night and brilliant ones that opened by day.

There was blossom in plenty all the way seawards, south of Santiago, to our first destination – Siboney and the historic chicken farm used as a camp by the combatants of the attack on the Moncada Fort. From this farm, according to the inscription, they departed on July 26th 1953 headed by Abel Santamaría and Fidel Castro, on a venture from which so many did not return.

Our second and much longer journey was to a range of mountains known as the Sierra Crystal. It was in this region in March 1958 that the Rebel Command sent Raúl Castro at the head of a column of sixty-eight men to open the Second Eastern Front, a campaign which proved one of the most successful. Soon we were in the cooler air of the high mountains, looking down upon coffee-covered hill tops with cattle grazing on the gentler slopes. Dotted about in the valley were small huts and farmsteads with here and there the washing hanging out among the banana trees, the mangoes and the water melons. On the outskirts of Mayari Ariba we stopped to have a word with a large party of weekend volunteer workers clearing weeds in a cane-field. Mayari is the great plateau which dominates the nickel-mining district of this region and near here the Castro children spent their childhood. Many hectares of land are now planted with fruit and vegetables and this is also an important timber-growing region but, like most of the mountain areas of Oriente, there are still many individual peasant farmers and today, as though to stress the fact, placards at the roadside remind the traveller of the coming congress of ANAP, the small farmers' national association.

After a further climb, we reached our destination on a plateau ringed round by the peaks of the Sierra Crystal. A muddy footpath led to a gate opening on to a small avenue of palms and a cottage on the walls of which was a plaque worded: *The headquarters of the Second Eastern Front Frank País August-December 1958 Column No. 6.* We waited for our guide in a small lobby furnished with the seats belonging to one of the planes captured from Batista's airforce. Photographs and correspondence were assembled on the walls to provide

199

visible proof that, despite statements to the contrary, the United States had supplied Batista with planes and weapons which were being used to bomb the area. After the bombardment of a village, some American residents from the near-by base were taken hostage by Raúl Castro's column and held by the guerrilla forces until their end was achieved and American assistance ended.

In the room of Vilma Espin, now president of the Federation of Cuban Women, I was shown photographs of a platoon of women guerrillas who like herself served with the column. Elsewhere a report from Raúl to Fidel Castro describes the first day's march, the tension arising from sixty hours without sleep and the march in the gruelling sun. Other entries describe the growing support from the people in the area, the setting up of a Committee of Revolutionary Farmers, the construction in the liberated territory of roads, telephones, radio, schools in which the Rebel Army men sometimes acted as tutors. There were also documents pertaining to a Farmers' Congress in September 1958 and the First Workers' Congress with delegates from the sugar mills. Pinned up prominently was an appeal to youth issued at the time. 'To all Cuban Youth, to all Latin American young people, to the youth of the world, save the youth of your brother country – youth who are giving all.'

Curator of the house is Omero Rodríguez, a peasant member of Column 6 born in 1917 and therefore in his forties at the time of the campaign. As a child, he said, he was taught to read and write by his father because at that time there was only one school in the whole area and most of the time the teacher was not there. Now in the Mayari region he told us besides one-class schools there were a primary school for five hundred pupils, a large secondary school, a technical school related to coffee growing, school workshops and a nursery school for infants in the surrounding villages. Previously there had been no hospital and once more I heard how patients had to be carried miles for treatment with personal memories of the sick dying on the way.

'Now we have a hospital,' he said. 'These days they don't

wait for you to get ill. They come house by house seeking out the children to vaccinate them.'

I asked about housing because en route we had seen many tumbledown houses and some bad conditions in the towns. He told us two hundred new houses had been built but we could see there were still housing problems in Cuba as in other countries. However, I learnt that in the new Cuba no one pays more in rent than ten per cent of the family income and some are now living rent free because by the Urban Reform Law rents continued to be paid up to a maximum period of fifteen years until the estimated construction cost of the house had been covered then the house became the tenant's to live in rent free. Now there is no private landlordism and no speculators to take advantage of housing shortages.

A small plantation surrounded the house stocked with coffee, grape-fruit, oranges, bananas, pineapples and papaya. Farmers locally, our guide explained, have their own branch of the Small Farmers' Association. They shared machinery and carried out many things jointly but they did not work as a collective. Each man farmed his own land.

I noticed a little queue of children lining up at the entrance to the museum, probably a school party. 'I have to tell the tale over and over again to the children who come to ask,' said Omero Rodríguez as we left him obviously enjoying his task. He would show the children the pictures and documents and they would see the past and the present through his eyes as we had done: a good a way as any, no more and no less partisan than the old history books but this time told from the standpoint of the workers and peasants and biased in favour of the Cuban Revolution.

POSTSCRIPT

As this goes to press, Cuba is working on a five year plan in a considerably improved situation in which her trading and diplomatic isolation from the rest of Latin America is fast ending. A majority of the members of the Organisation of American States have just voted to end the trade embargo that has operated against Cuba since 1961. Moreover a British trade delegation has this year visited Cuba and, according to press reports, there are possibilities of large scale trade between the two countries. Similar links are being made around the world and in the United States itself opinion is growing in favour of resumed relations with Cuba. At the same time, Cuba is now a full member of COMECON (the socialist nearest equivalent to the Common Market) and events leading to the downfall of the Allende government in Chile have reinforced Cuban policy concerning the maintenance of vigilance and a high level of military preparedness.

With the economy on a sounder basis, Cuba in the 'seventies has been turning its attention to the important task of creating new representative institutions to replace the provisional framework of government appointed by decree during the early years of revolutionary rule. Questions concerning these new laws and institutions of people's power were being thrashed out in all those conferences that during my stay in Cuba were either happening or about to happen: conferences of farmers, secondary school pupils, women, medical workers, teachers, trade unionists, armed forces, young communists, writers and artists and musicians.

Among the first fruits of these discussions has been a unique election experiment in Matanzas Province. In keeping with Cuba's present method of testing each new step in practice and learning from people's reactions, it was decided

202

to hold elections for what are called Assemblies of People's Power in one province so that based on this experience any hitches that might arise could be corrected before application to the whole country in 1976. Before then there will be further conferences including the first national congress of the Communist Party of Cuba since the revolution, to evaluate the lessons of the whole experiment.

The question arises as to why all this has not happened before. Deputy Prime Minister Raúl Castro in a tutorial with about a thousand newly-elected delegates to People's Power in Matanzas explained that in the early years of rapid change they were faced with threats on all sides to Cuba's very existence. Not only had all efforts to be concentrated on survival but they often had to make very swift decisions and this situation required a state apparatus where legislative, administrative and executive powers were concentrated in one body. Also shortages for the first decade were such that even if it would have been correct to set up representative bodies of people's power, it was feared that they would not be able to function properly and so become discredited. Added to all this, he said there was 'a certain lack of experience and understanding on the part of many of us regarding the importance of these organisations and the role they have to play . . . Nevertheless, the state is and has always been an essentially democratic state of the humble, for the humble, by the humble.' The stated aim in setting up the new People's Power Assemblies is to disperse the centralisation of power and consequential bureaucracy that had grown up in the provisional state structures during the first decade of revolutionary rule.

This ability to evaluate a situation in public consultation with the people without sweeping anything under the carpet seems to me the most salutary and attractive feature of the Cuban Revolution.

There is an interesting reference to the Matanzas election experiment by Dr I. M. Fraser, Dean of Mission of Selly Oak Colleges, Birmingham, in a wide-ranging report of a visit he recently paid to Cuba as a delegate from the World Council of Churches to the Annual Assembly of the Council of Protestant Churches of Cuba from which he has kindly given me permission to quote. He describes a consultation with Mr José Carneado, Head of the Department of Sciences, Culture and Education of the Central Committee of the Communist Party.

'Here was no propaganda exercise. Quite briefly he started by indicating the problems they were facing, the means they were taking to handle these, and drew us into conversation, inviting our own reactions. We were all free to raise whatever questions we wanted. I used the opportunity to press a personal question. It concerned the city of Matanzas which we visited, which had been chosen for a pilot scheme . . . The slogan everywhere in that city was "Power to the People" or "People's Power is real Power". The local government had been elected by a free vote of the people for candidates who did not need to be members of the Communist Party. The candidates had to be known locally and locally accountable – the idea was that they should not become bureaucrats passing the buck from desk to desk or commission to commission; but persons who would be directly responsible to an area, who had to deal personally with the needs of people in that area. Biographies of every candidate were issued to every voter. The Council which was elected was responsible for industrial development, education, housing and community life in that area, within nationally established priorities (as is the case in Britain). Over ninety per cent of the population voted.

'It is a sign of a way Cuba may take from this point on. Those who had visited Cuba some years ago remarked on the more relaxed and confident contemporary feel of the whole governmental operation. The revolution had proved itself. It was irreversible. It had established itself in the minds of the people. Over the last few years, the development of communications with more countries had helped in a greater openness. Mr Careado was a sign in himself. convinced, open, free in relationship and conversation.'

Clearly housing in the last two years has made big strides

for Dr Fraser reports that people told him with joy how the shanty towns outside the cities had been swept away and that everywhere there were signs of flats and houses being built.

Dr Fraser's report raises some questions which, whether or not one agrees with his viewpoint, are of great interest. He believes a revolutionary system when a certain point is reached in its development, gets either more rigid or more human, and he asks which way will be taken by Cuba? He sees as hopeful straws in the wind. a) the evidence of constant experimentation, the approach being 'to do what looks appropriate, evaluate it, learn lessons from it, and then plan in the light of that experience, taking risks of the imagination'; b) freer contacts with other countries and relaxation of the trade embargoes contributing to greater openness; c) the fact that no political prisoners have been jailed in the past two years; d) the spirit of the people with their Latin-American flair for living 'that will not be dragooned' and the parallel flexibility of government.

Cuba revisited

Dr Fraser's report ends with the conclusion that 'There is something fundamentally right about Cuba', and this just about summarises my own feelings after a short return visit to Cuba in March-April of 1975. This time I stayed in Old Havana, much nearer to the everyday business of Cuban life but still only a few minutes away from the Malecon and the Caribbean Sea. This area of Havana was without water except from water-carts when I arrived, a serious matter in tropical heat but useful in revealing how authorities and people coped. There was the fullest possible public explanation, giving technical details with illustrations of the precise nature of the problem and daily news bulletins of progress in dealing with it. I myself was able to read the details on a neighbouring CDR notice board. Minimum essential supplies were pumped in by water-cart whose arrival was greeted by groups of neighbours using inventive methods to wind up extra buckets on improvised pulleys to top flats. Because of worn-out water and sewage equipment as well as overcrowding, it is planned to rebuild parts of this district entirely, but it is a fascinating area, full of the street games of children in the evening and at eight in the morning alive with cherry red berets and blue and white pioneer scarves as school children make their way to primary school. And just up the street, when dawn turns the pinnacles of houses pink and yellow, one can sometimes surprise a solitary ibis feeding in rock pools at the sea's edge.

Avenue Galiano and the shopping centre near the hotel was a new experience. Some of its 'people's stores' are spacious with sliding staircases from floor to floor. The colourful decor of shops large and small is designed by a team of artists and most now display a limited selection of off ration goods. Some former shops have been turned into workshops where from the street one can see guitars being made or diesel parts. Others are trade union headquarters and small group meetings in full view add to the impression remarked on by other visitors that being in Cuba is rather like being part of a perpetual general meeting. A refreshment bar serving ice cold beer was a popular place for relaxing after work as was a café serving snacks, all much more readily available than two years ago. But the most frequented place in the Avenue was a small square where on seats under the shade of trees, by sunlight and lamplight, senior citizens and others conversed or read the newspaper on sale at the book kiosk at the corner of the square. Here little queues were always forming. One day while sitting in the square, I counted three hundred queuing for *Bohemia* – a general cultural-cum-political-cum-family magazine. The literacy campaign has swollen Cuba's reading public and its thirst for reading material continues to grow. Directly new books are announced long queues begin to form. Books are cheap in Cuba and, although problems of equipment created by the embargo still make their presence felt, the Cuban Book Institute in 1974 published twenty-nine million book units – seventy per cent of which were educational.

It was as a guest of the Book Institute that I paid a second visit to Cuba. My companions once more were young people: Nancy, a fully trained librarian with a small daughter, who is director of the foreign relations department of this giant state concern and is also studying languages; Daniel, a Young Communist from the same department and sharing responsibility; and Horacio, a translator of medical books. All three were in their twenties or early thirties. They confirmed my earlier impression of Cuba's young 'responsibles': dedicated to their work and to the revolution (to a point sometimes near physical exhaustion), able to look critically at themselves, internationally minded with wide cultural interests including the culture of other countries, a sense of humour and 'a flair for living'.

There are plans to widen Cuba's main highway. A greater width had been budgeted for in Machado's day but the minister responsible decided to construct it at its present breadth and pocket the difference. Along its length west to lovely Soreo at the foot of the Rosario Mountains of Pinar del Río or east to Matanzas and Veradero beach, one saw evidence everywhere of the new housing construction mentioned by Dr Fraser. The policy is to build fairly small communities complete with social services – educational, recreational and environmental – requiring minimum travel. Prefabricated methods of construction are mainly used and apartment blocks, of modest height, seem to predominate, at least in Havana Province. In those I saw, adventurous colour and variety of texture prevented the monotony sometimes associated with this type of building. More than six hundred of these new communities have so far been built.

During my second stay in Cuba, a meeting of unaligned countries was taking place in Havana and *Granma* carried verbatim reports of Fidel Castro's speech in which he urged the oil producing states to maintain solidarity by giving priority in credits to those parts of the underdeveloped world still crippled by the grossly unjust terms of world trade.

(Cuba, of course, continues to receive her oil from the plentiful resources of the Soviet Union according to collateral agreements entered into long ago at the beginning of the American blockade.)

In conversation, the new family code was a frequent talking point – not surprisingly since Cuba is the first country to legislate in this way for equality in the home. The effect of the code will, no doubt, be mainly educational but my friends felt that already the public debate had speeded up the change of attitudes and in the last few years there had been profound changes in women's own attitude to their role in society, one outward sign of which was the several hundred women construction workers helping in every aspect of the work of the 'mini-brigades' in the port of Havana.

I noticed that the passage from Fidel Castro's speech to the congress of the Federation of Cuban Women chosen for display by our local group was the one in which he said: 'If women are physically weaker, if women must be mothers, if on top of their social obligations, if on top of their work, they carry the weight of reproduction and childbearing, of giving birth to every human being who enters the world, and if they bear the physical and biological sacrifices these functions bring with them, it is just that women should be given all the consideration they deserve in society.' Progress was expected to be uneven; old habits will not change overnight, particularly among older couples some of whom may be happy with their present relationship like the skilled worker and his wife of retiring age who said to me: 'My wife says she prefers the kitchen to herself and so you see how she spoils me.' But it is not just a matter of generation for at breakfast in the hotel, a transport worker probably in his fifties, opened up the subject himself by saying: 'In Latin America, men are up there and women are down there but we had a very good congress at the end of last year that will help to change all that.'

The new family code came into practice on 8th of March 1975, International Women's Year. In it socialist Cuba's concept of the family is defined as 'based on the fundamental consideration that the family constitutes an entity in which social and personal interests are present and closely linked in view of the fact that it is the elementary cell of society and, as such, contributes to its development and plays an important role in the upbringing of tof the new generations. Moreover, as the centre for relations of common existence between men and women and between them and their children and between all of them and their relatives, it meets deep-rooted human needs in the social field and in the field of affection for the individual.'

According to Blas Roca of the Law Commission, the new legislation frees marriage from the economic, almost commercial character of the civil contract which prevailed in the former code, when legalised marriage as the general rule was associated mainly with the wealthier classes. The new Code defines marriage as 'the voluntarily established union between a man and a woman who are legally fit to form such a union, in order to live together'. Citizens can get married at eighteen at their own choice, or under that age in exceptional cases and with parents permission if the girl is at least fourteen and the boy sixteen. Now when a couple decides to marry, they are read the following articles of the family code which deal with the rights and duties of the partners: 'Marriage is established with equal rights and duties for both partners . . . Both partners must care for the family they have created and each partner must cooperate with the other in the education, upbringing and guidance of the children according to the principles of socialist morality. They must participate to the extent of their capacities and possibilities, in the running of the home, and cooperate so that it will develop in the best possible way . . . The partners must help meet the needs of the family they have created with their marriage, each according to his or her ability and financial status. However, if one of them only contributes by working at home and caring for the children, the other partner must contribute to this support alone, without prejudice to his duty of cooperating in the above mentioned work and care . . . Both partners have the right to practice their profession or skill and they have the duty of helping each other and cooperating in order to make this possible and to study and improve their knowledge. However, they must always see to it that home life is organised in such a way that these activities are coordinated with their fulfillment of obligations posed by the Code.'

Thirteen articles then elaborate very precisely the principle that 'the economic basis of matrimony will be the joint property of goods'. On divorce Article 51 states: 'Divorce will take effect by common agreement when the court determines that there are factors which have led the marriage to lose its meaning for the partners and for the children and thus for society as a whole', the aim being to free the couple obtaining a divorce from the situation in which 'one spouse tries to belittle the other, without benefit to anyone and with obvious harm to the children who are led to have a hateful image of their parents or one of them.'

Section 2 of the Code is entitled 'Relationships between Parents and Children.' It states that 'All children are equal and they have equal rights and duties with regard to their parents regardless of the latter's civil status . . . Children are obliged to respect, show consideration for and help their parents, and respect them while under parental control.' Parents' rights and duties are then enumerated at some length in relation to a stable home, health, recreation, education and training for useful citizenship 'in the spirit of internationalism . . . and respect for their country's values'. Parents are exhorted to arouse the respect of their children by their attitude toward them, 'setting straight adequately and moderately' those children under their care.

During the nationwide discussion, ninety-eight per cent of those who took part approved the new Code, and four thousand suggestions and comments were made pertaining to three quarters of its one hundred and sixty-six articles. Among the two percent not approving were a few women's groups but the great majority were enthusiastically in favour of what is described in Cuba as 'an important step in the struggle to achieve true equality of all citizens, men and women, black and white, in society and in personal life'.

210

In a final visit to Santiago de Cuba I saw this green and leafy city for the first time by night – its spectacular sports city, the sculptured 'Forest of the Dead' impressive by floodlight, the 26th July school replacing the blood-stained citadel of the Moncada (Plate VII) and the strangely beautiful cemetery on the hill where José Martí and all Cuba's long line of heroes and heroines lie buried. In the heat of the day, we visited the shady valleys of the mango-growing country and drank cooling juice overlooking ancient trees. But it is the people I met in Oriente I want most to remember. We talked late into the night with three Cubans from the new Oriente Publishing House. They were experienced industrial workers who had entered university through the worker-peasant faculties to qualify at degree level as journalists. They spoke of the stimulating effect on writers when, after meeting national requirements, publishing could be geared to the needs of a region – in this case to the mines, farms, factories and the children of the mountainous province of Oriente where a third of Cuba's population lives. We discussed the value of decentralisation in avoiding bureaucracy, and, while warning me not to get an exaggerated idea of achievements to date, they outlined plans to extend the present distribution network (seventy bookshops scattered over 33,000 square kilometres) to remote country regions by travelling library van, mule transport and if necessary by foot.

Beside the present and the future, we spoke of the past and the complex combination of factors, often oversimplified in books, that led to victory in 1959. the equal and complementary contribution of city and mountain – urban resistance and guerrilla action – the quality of the leadership and the involvement of the mass of the people in struggle.

It is in this matter of involvement that perhaps one notices the biggest development in the 'seventies. On the very last day of my Cuban journey I found on the wall notice-board of a block of flats opposite the sea the following quotation

211

from José Martí: 'The fact escapes the despots that it is the suffering masses that are the true leaders of the Revolution.' These street wall-newspapers are in some ways a barometer of the stages reached in the revolution and the choice of quotation seemed to me significant – a reflection of the self-confidence, deepened involvement and increased reliance on the people and their organisations that a traveller senses in Cuba today.